140351
AUG '06
JAN 12
JUL - 2015
1424

Reefs, Wrecks and Rigs

Diver's Guide to the Northern Gulf of Mexico

Tom Bailey

D0869050

Seacoast Pu
Birmingham, Alabama

Copyright © 1993 by Tom Bailey

All rights reserved. No part of this book may be reproduced or transmitted in any form or by any means without permission in writing from the publisher. Of course, writers of periodicals and reviews may feel free to comment on and to quote briefly from the book.

Published by Seacoast Publishing Inc., P.O. Box 26492, Birmingham, Alabama 35226.

Manufactured in the United States of America.

ISBN: 1-878561-18-9

Contents

140351

T 39696

Triggerfish nibble at crustaceans and other growth covering crossmembers of an oil rig, while a jack cruises in the background

Photo courtesy of Captain J's Dive Shop, Destin, Fla.

Spadefish and grunts drift in and out of an automobile, now part of an artificial reef off Pensacola, Fla.

Photo courtesy of Gulf Coast Pro Dive, Pensacola, Fla.

Introduction

In 1983 I wrote Diver's Guide to the Alabama-Florida Gulf—a decent guidebook to diving opportunities along the northern gulf rim from Mexico Beach, Florida, to Gulf Shores, Alabama.

Two things happened:

1. Before the book could sell out, this dynamic industry changed dramatically with a number of new shops opening. And equipment improvements made many of the photos obsolete.

2. Sportsmen developed literally hundreds of new dive spots—some created as artificial reefs or wrecks, while others were newly discovered reefs that had been there all along.

Not only had that original territory matured and grown, a new, dynamic and very different dive environment was growing in popularity. Reports about oil rig diving off Louisiana and Mississippi were spreading along the coast.

A third phenomenon that gave me heart was the recent restrictions placed on the size and number of fish that sportsmen could harvest. For a time in the early and mid 1980s, several species—amberjack, snappers, mackerel and grouper, in particular—were badly depleated by overharvesting.

Since those restrictions were put in place, the highly-sought species have rebounded quickly. A reef is a dramatic sight for a diver any time, but one with an abundant population of sea life is even more breathtaking.

As dive shops throughout the area have matured, they have developed larger and larger repertoires of dive opportunities—reefs, wrecks, artificial reefs, oil and gas rigs, fresh-water cavern dives, night reef dives, snorkeling trips for novices, lobstering, shell collecting, tropicals collecting, underwater photography, and all offered with an extremely high expertise level.

So, here, 10 years after the first northern gulf diving guide was published, a successor takes its place—broader in scope to alert divers to diving off Mississippi and Louisiana, more thorough to highlight newly developed and newly discovered dive spots off the Florida panhandle and Alabama coasts, and more complete in guiding divers through entertainment, lodging and dining opportunities in each location.

My hope is that this book will help you discover and enjoy the growing dive opportunities as much as I have enjoyed discovering them over the past decade.

Happy diving.

—Tom Bailey

*A diver descends into the crystal pool of Cypress Spring,
less than an hour north of Destin and Panama City, Fla.*
Photo courtesy of Harold Vickers, Cypress Spring

Geography

The Gulf of Mexico is a great pond; its shoreline stretching from Mexico's Yucatan Peninsula to Florida's southernmost tip. Its outlet is through the Caribbean to the Atlantic Ocean.

This pond covers almost 700,000 square miles, is 800 miles long and 1,100 miles wide. It has a 3,000 mile coastline and is 12,700 feet deep at its deepest point.

An arm of the Gulf Stream—that huge river current of ocean water sweeping through the Atlantic—swirls through the gulf, bringing a constant flow of clear, clean warm water to this giant pond. And that oceanic stream of water—called the Loop Current—comes closest to land along the northern gulf coast.

With it comes sea life that makes the area so special—from tropical fishes normally associated with waters far south to the giant Blue Marlin. In addition, the stream brings the White Marlin, Wahoo, the clawless Florida lobsters and other sea creatures that ride the current out of the Caribbean to make their homes in and around the fine sands.

The sand of the eastern half of this region is a curiosity—pure white, almost sugar-like both in color and consistency. Mostly quartz, the sand grains are extremely pure and fine, free of mud and other impurities. Beaches of the region are ranked among the best in the world.

The western half of the region is a marked contrast. From Mobile Bay to the mouth of the Mississippi River, numerous rivers dump millions of gallons of murky fresh water and silt from half the continent into the gulf.

The shoreline is dotted with barrier islands, salt marshes and muddy shorelines. Even reaching the shore can be a chore. But off this huge delta are massive oil fields. Standing in the gulf and drawing that oil from the sea floor are huge oil rigs—close to 3,800 of them—and each has formed a dramatic sea life habitat where none had existed before.

But back to the eastern half. The sand lies in a thick blanket and extends for miles along the gulf floor. To the bather's delight it is so gently sloping that a person can wade out for great distances in many spots. It is barrier free and on most days free of significant current.

Along the shore, the sand has built up into two sand bars paralleling the beach, leaving a small shallow trough very near the beach, a sand bar, a deeper trough and then another sand bar—sometimes called a green reef. After that the bottom begins its steady drop to blue water.

Interrupting the sand's smooth to gently rolling decline to the cliffs that lie miles out to sea are potholes, and small limestone and coral reefs where fish, shells, fishermen and divers gather. The reefs and rocks wander in and out from shore in a more or less east-west pattern.

To the west of Mobile Bay is a dramatically different coastline. Barrier Islands hold murky waters flowing into the gulf from rivers and creeks close to shore.

Thousands of years of freshwater flow from those rivers has dumped silt into the gulf that has turned into land and left that part of the gulf with a soft mud bottom. The tremendous flow of nutrients into the gulf and the low wetlands created by the flow has created massive nurseries for sea life. Shrimping, oystering and fishing communities dot the coastline, taking advantage of the shelters just inside the mouth of these rivers and of the rich sea life drawn to the nutrients.

The soft shallow muddy bottom extends for a dozen miles or more offshore before bumping into the wild and uninhabited barrier islands.

Beyond the islands are where the true gulf waters begin. Outside those islands flows the Loop Current, clear waters and major geologic formations that drop to the depths.

The Gulf of Mexico probably was formed as the American and

African continents separated millions of years ago. The current shorelines are but one of many that have existed through the years as water levels rose and sank. At times, shorelines were far north of their present locations with water covering large parts of Louisiana, Mississippi, Alabama and Florida. At other times, shorelines were far offshore and what now are limestone ledges were shallow, luxurious reefs.

One of those ancient shorelines lies near the dropoffs of the northern gulf's major geologic formations—the DeSoto and Mississippi canyons. The DeSoto Canyon lies nearest Destin, Pensacola and Gulf Shores, 40 or 50 miles out. The Mississippi Canyon lies a similar distance off the tip of Louisiana.

The rough edges and cliffs of these canyons are home for many game fish and are funnels for clear gulf waters to wash into near-shore areas and provide the crisp visibility that divers enjoy in these areas.

Hundreds of Vermilion snapper swarm over the sunken tug Heron, which lies upside down in a sunken Navy landing craft off Pensacola, Fla.

Photo courtesy of Scuba Shack, Pensacola

The Weather

The Gulf of Mexico makes weather.

Each day millions of gallons of water evaporate from its surface and struggle northward until they drop from a summer thundershower or as winter snow or sleet.

No matter the season, the gulf air coats the beach areas with a salty layer—a translucent film that seems to stick to everything it touches. Take precautions. Wash your car, giving particular attention to spraying the fender wells, under bumpers and other places where salty sand can hide, as soon as you get home from a dive trip.

Wash fishing tackle, dive gear and other beach supplies after each use. Everything will last longer with a good dousing of fresh water.

While some complain of summer mugginess, the summertime highs do not, in fact, reach the extremes common to areas far inland. A 100-degree day is rare.

While the weather is relatively mild even in the depths of winter, there are distinctive seasons along the northern gulf—far from the seasonal sameness of south Florida.

During summer, daytime highs average in the mid-90s, kept from going higher by prevailing sea breezes that bring cooling air off the gulf each day. Those summer breezes give way to northerly winds which prevail in winter months. Summer night temperatures range from 70 to 75 degrees.

Winter months have a wider variety of temperatures. From November to March it is not unusual to have a low of 40 (and once in a while in the 30s) and highs in the 70s on the same day. Rare winter readings hit the low 80s, but more frequently are in the 60s or low 70s. While low temperatures in winter will drop to freezing once in a while, the temperature does not remain below freezing all day even on the coldest days.

For the year, the sun shines on this part of the coast 65 to 67 percent of the time, with clear skies about 55 percent of the time in winter and about 75 percent of the time from May through October. Stated another way, the sun shines on this region as least part of the day on an average of 343 days each year.

Summer breezes during the day can range from 10 to 15 miles per hour, falling to below 10 miles per hour at night. The exception being stronger, gusty winds near thundershowers. Winds can vary more in winter, and at times are particularly strong during the late fall and early srping when cold and warm fronts clash.

Much of the sea action is based on winds, with seas usually four feet or less when winds are 15 miles per hour or less.

Average annual rainfall is between 55 and 60 inches—about like the rest of the southeast—with most of that rain coming during the spring and summer. Most comes during the late afternoon or early evening in short, intense thundershowers.

The showers can be both a curse and blessing. They are welcome relief from the afternoon heat. They also bring intense lightning. Heavier thunderstorms can spawn tornadoes and waterspouts, which are tornadoes formed over water.

A heavy thunderstorm can swamp a small boat, and a waterspout can smash a big one. Boaters should watch the weather and make for port when thunderstorms develop. Divers should get out of the water during thundershowers.

In late summer and early fall, hurricanes develop in the Atlantic and occasionally spin their way into the gulf. While these storms are rare, when they hit the area they cause major destruction. These are huge cyclic storms, with heavy rains and winds that can reach 200 miles an hour, swirling around a calm center.

If one is moving into the gulf, monitor weather forecasts closely. If the storm is coming ahywhere close, forget your dive trip until it has passed. And don't wait near the beach for it to pass. If forecasters urge you to move inland, do so quickly. Hurricanes usually move slowly. There will be time to get out of the way.

But mostly, the gulf is calm, with an occasional chop of two to three feet. For two thirds of the year, maybe a little more, the water is warm--in the mid 80s during summer months, dipping into the 70s in the late fall, into the 50s by late winter, then back into the 60s and 70s during the spring.

A few people, particularly some of those from Canada and northern states who are accustomed to colder climates, swim in the gulf year around—any time the air temperature warms enough to allow them to wear bathing suits.

However, most people from the southeast find the water uncomfortable chilly from November until late April or May, and wear wetsuits when diving.

Of course, there are good sun-bathing days year around, and because of the reflective white sand, sunburn must be guarded against in every season.

Summer dress need be only the lightest of clothes. Many persons spend entire summer vacations in shorts and short-sleeve shirts. Winters require sweaters, along with a light- to medium-weight jacket.

Caps or hats always are a good idea for guarding against the sun and to protect you from breezy weather.

Rubble from Hathaway Bridge that once spanned St. Andrews Bay, now form artificial reefs from Mexico Beach to Panama City. All hold significant life.

Photo courtesy of Tanya Murphy

Port St. Joe/ Mexico Beach

The Area

Just before the beach highway, U.S. 98 makes a northward swing toward Florida's big bend and the broad muddy flats characterizing that area, divers find these last ports where the shore is sugar-white beach, and dive spots within easy reach just off shore.

They anchor the eastern end of our dive region, and while they may be a bit quieter than the hurly-burly of Panama City Beach, these are quite well-developed resort communities that include nearby dive facilties, restaurants and lodging.

From east or west, the communities lie on U.S. 98, which for much of the 10 miles between the two is right against the shoreline.

Mexico Beach has protected docks along a channel that leads directly into the gulf, and tourism, fishing and other shore-related activities form the base of the economy.

Port St. Joe, on the other hand, has a varied economy, with the St. Joe paper company's huge mill on the bay strong evidence of the economic base. Chemical companies and a fishery also contribute.

Where to Stay

A variety of motels and condominiums right along the shore in

Mexico Beach, St. Joe Beach, Cape San Blas and Indian Pass present options for all budgets.

And, while the beach resorts hold their own with others in the area, there are additional opportunities for those who are looking for something a little more secluded. Because this area is not so heavily developed, there are rustic cabins for rent in several areas.

There also are campgrounds in Mexico Beach, at St. Joseph State Park and Indian Pass.

Where to Eat

Great seafood is available throughout the region, and in a region where seafood is part of the economy you will find a number of locations offering their own recipes, prepared with care and pride.

A couple of the more popular ones are Henderson's Restaurant & Produce and Indian Pass Rawbar.

A half hour south are the towns of Apalachicola and Eastpoint, home to the region's largest oystering operation. Many visitors make a trip to buy unshucked oysters by the bushel, and other fresh seafood to create their own "fisherman's platter."

Many of the commercial operations operate their own retail markets right on the shore where their boats dock.

When You Aren't Diving

The usual water stuff is available, and both salt- and fresh-water fishing among the best anywhere. Charter boats are available in both Mexico Beach and Port St. Joe, where inshore and offshore fishing is excellent.

In addition, some of the largest largemouth bass caught in America come from nearby Dead Lakes. Fish camps offer services.

In season, this area also is one of Florida's most popular hunting areas. Sportsmen seek deer, turkey, squirrel, wild hogs, rabbits, quail, marsh hens, doves, ducks and geese.

Other attractions include Constitution State Monument and Museum has exhibits of the area's early history and the story of Florida's first constitutional convention which took place on the site in 1838.

Confederate Salt Works processed 150 bushes of salt a day from sea water. It was destroyed by a Union ship.

T.H. Stone Memorial/St. Joseph Peninsula State Park teems with wildlife and marine life. Park visitors can crab, scallop, collect shells, skin and scuba dive, water ski, hike and picnic. There are camping facilities, a boat ramp, boat basin and canoe rentals. Wildlife includes 209 species of birds, gray fox, raccoon, deer, skunk and bobcat.

For more information on the Mexico Beach/Port St. Joe areas, write or call:

Mexico Beach Chamber of Commerce
P.O. Box 13382
Mexico Beach, FL 32410
(904)648-8196 or (800)239-9553

Port St. Joe/Gulf County Chamber of Commerce
P.O. Box 964
Port St. Joe, FL 32456
(904)227-1223

Mexico Beach/Port St. Joe Diving

There is one dive shop serving this area. It is a well-established shop, with full service and offering trips to a number of sites throughout this part of the gulf, including what many call the region's premier wreck dive—the Empire Mica, a British tanker that was torpedoed by a German submarine during World War II.

The local shop is:

Captain Black's Dive Center
301 Monument Ave. (Highway 98)
Port St. Joe, FL 32456
(904)229-6330

Shore Dives

The shoreline here is must like the rest of the Florida panhandle, with a gently sloping sand bottom and rolling sand bars. Some snorkelers find several species of surf fish interesting to look at, but this is not the diving that brings folks to the region.

Scallop beds
While this may not be a classic dive, many divers do take

advantage of the huge and prolific scallop beds in St. Joseph Bay. Bay scallops may be harvested in summer, but make sure the season is open before taking them.

Sharks Hole

While this shell wall is just off the tip of St. Joseph Peninsula, you really need a boat to get there since there are no roads. The wall is just inside the bay and was formed by tidal currents. Wall height ranges from three to 30 feet.

Open Gulf

Wreck and artificial reef diving is among the area's most popular, and sea life is abundant throughout—particularly several species of reef fish.

Wrecks

Lumber Ship Vamar

Just over two miles out, this 170-foot lumber boat is but scattered remains in slightly more than 20 feet of water just north of the channel. Tropicals, octopus and small reef fish are common. 14142.9/46830.5

Kaiser

This tug boat went down more than 60 years ago, less than two miles northwest of the sea buoy. Significant wreckage remains. Depth is approximately 45 feet. A number of reef species are frequently seen.

Schooner Thelma

Some ribs and other debris remain from this ship that went down more than 50 years ago. It is about 20 miles west of Cape San Blas. 13902.0/46731.1

Audrey

Remains of a tug boat are west of Cape San Blas in 100 feet of water. Reef species are prevalent. 13916.1/46721.1

Empire Mica

This 465-foot tanker went down June 3, 1942, having drifted

and burned for 24 hours before going down in just over 100 feet of water. The ship is showing some age, but the two torpedo holes still are visible in the ship's side. Exceptional visibility, and abundant sea life. 14023.5/46489.6

Barges

Like most other locations, this area also has its share of these popular artificial reefs. They include:

Bill's Barge is six miles west of the Port St. Joe sea buoy in 80 feet of water. It is showing some deterioration, and holds a good fish population. 14059.1/46836.8

Davis Barge is southeast of St. Andrews Bay old pass, northwest of Mexico Beach. The barge has been there since the 1950s, lying in about 50 feet of water. 14115.7/46916.2

Barrier Dunes barge lies just offshore of the St. Joseph Peninsula in about 30 feet of water. The 170-foot barge sank in the late 1980s. It holds mostly smaller game fish and tropicals. 14114.9/ 46741.6

Sunken Barge is but three and a half miles west of the sea buoy in about 70 feet of water. It is said to hold good populations of game fish.

Gatewood Barge is six miles southwest of the sea buoy in 80 feet of water. It is listed among the wrecks regularly visited by Captain Black's. Loran coordinates were not available.

Landing Craft (LST)

The military landing craft sank in the early 1960s about 11 miles south of the sea buoy in 90 feet of water. Lots of game fish and shells reported. The craft is about 75 feet long and rises more than 15 feet off the bottom. 14062.0/46719.0

Artificial Reefs

Box Cars

A large and well developed artificial reef site that includes not only a couple of railroad box cars, but car bodies, tires and rubble. The area is three miles northwest of the sea buoy. 14116.6/46845.5

Bridge Rubble

A deck from the Hathaway Bridge reef building project, this

concrete and steel rubble is in 60 feet of water and only a half mile from the box cars. 14112.6/46845.5

Another section of the bridge is about 10 miles west of the sea buoy in 100 feet of water. This is one of the large spans, rising 30 feet or more off the bottom. 14003.8/46790.3

Shrimper's Junkpile

A large area of various junk—ranging from cars to boats and appliances. Holds lots of fish. About two miles southwest of the sea buoy. 14104.0/46815.0

Eddy's

An artificial reef funded by the city of Port St. Joe and the state, beginning in 1989. The hundred-square-yard area is in just over 40 feet of water. Material includes 250 dumpsters. It is within two miles of the sea buoy. 14115.8/46804.3

J.C. Reef

This artificial site includes a lot of concrete pilings, that create a relatively low profile but hold a good amount of sea life, perhaps attributable to the fact that the reef was started 25 years ago. 14115.7/46804.1

Cape San Blas Lighthouse

The remains of an old brick lighthouse are in 25 feet of water a quarter mile off Cape San Blas. 14113.2/46679.1

Mexico Beach Site

A large area of wreckage that includes car bodies, tires, metal junk in 50 to 55 feet of water. 14116.6/46845.5

Mexico Beach Concrete Reef

This concrete rubble is in about 60 feet of water and is only about a mile west of the Kaiser wreck. 14112.5/46840.9

Captain Black Sites

Captain Black's Dive Center also reports running regular dive trips to spots named The Gatewood, Catherine's Kitchen, Capt. Jim and Captain Kato. Loran coordinates were not available for these spots, and understandably so. It is reported that the Gatewood is a 70-

foot barge in 80 feet of water that Captain Black's is maintaining at its own expense and where spearfishing is not allowed. Good visibility.

Catherine's Kitchen is an artificial reef in 85 feet of water and near the Gatewood. It consists of box cars, tires and metal debris. Capt. Jim is wreckage of a shrimp boat in 110 feet of water, standing 30 feet off the bottom. It is more than 20 miles from the sea buoy. Captain Kato is another shrimp boat, west of Cape San Blas in 65 feet of water. It holds a lot of sea life, according to reports.

Vermilion Snapper (Mingo), grunts and Amberjack swarm over a shipwreck off Panama City, Fla., a scene common to wrecks of the Florida Panhandle.

Photo courtesy of Davy Jones Locker, Mobile, Ala.

CAPTAIN BLACK'S
JETTY DIVE STORE
ST. ANDREW'S STATE PARK

Dolphin Encounters

"Meet me at St. Andrew's"

**Swim, Snorkel, & Play
with the Dolphins
in the wild!**
*FOR RESERVATIONS
& INFORMATION*

904-233-0197

CAPTAIN BLACK'S
DIVE CENTER

*"SHIPWRECK
CAPITAL
OF
FLORIDA"*

EMPIRE MICA
TRIPS

*Plus over 20 other
Natural
&
Artificial Wreck
&
Reef Sites*

Port St. Joe, FL 32456
(35 Miles East of Panama City)

904-229-6330

Panama City

The Area

The Panama City area—which includes the city of Panama City and the adjoining resort communities of Panama City Beach, Laguna Beach and Sunnyside—is a fully-developed resort center.

Visitors will find lodging of every variety and price range. There is a wide range of dining opportunities, and water sports are a centerpiece of this region that boasts the world's most beautiful beaches.

Actually Panama City's beaches—as virtually all those of the Florida panhandle—are indeed among the world's most beautiful beaches. The gently sloping shore, pure white sands, generally mild currents and clear water have garnered top marks from several groups that rate the quality of such things.

The tourism folks bill the area as a family-oriented vacation destination. And it is, with all sorts of family recreation, excursions and parks available.

But for thousands of middle aged Alabamians and Georgians who spent their teen summers at the now demolished "Hangout," Panama City was a place for sewing wild oats, coming of age and general teen-age carrying on.

Maybe that has toned down some through the years. But there still is more than enough party life to satisfy the most demanding of visitors. Panama City offers some top flight beach club entertainment—and some probably that "family" vacationers will consider off limits.

The cultures seem to coexist comfortably, however. Parts of the beach are quiet, laid back, and catering to mom, pop and the kids. Other sections are obviously for the younger crowd that can stay up later and party longer.

A single drive down the strip—the U.S. 98 beach route—will leave no doubt about which area is for which group. If you are making arrangements by telephone and never have visited Panama City, just ask the reservationist about your location. Most will gladly help make sure you find your way to the right spot for your lifestyle.

As for a place to stay:

Luxury condominiums are available on the beach front and several bay locations. Most offer pools, and some include health clubs, golf resorts, tennis courts, game rooms and other recreation facilities.

Hotels and motels also are available beach front, bay front and inland. Of course, the further off the beach you are the lower the price, generally speaking.

More than 16,000 motel, hotel and condominium units are available.

In addition there are a number of RV resorts and campgrounds. St. Andrews State Park is one of Florida's most frequently used campgrounds, often completely filled in summer. However, a number of campgrounds—beachside, bayside and inland—usually can accommodate campers on short notice.

There are several overnight dock facilities for boaters.

Panama City does frequently fill up, especially during spring holidays and through the summer. Thus, it is advisable to call ahead for reservations.

For reservation information call 1-904-234-3193.

So now you're hungry.

You're at the beach, so what do you expect? Corn fed beef? As a matter of fact Panama City does boast a couple of the best steak houses you will find anywhere.

But, yes, seafood is the specialty. The best seafood houses. Ask around and watch the long lines at dinner time each evening. A little asking around and you will get more great suggestions than you can get to in two or three vacations.

In a resort this well developed, you can find anything you

want—even a great steak.

You also can get world-class gourmet meals at several restaurants, great local seafood just about anywhere, family-style family-owned or chain restaurants or hamburgers from the pervasive fast-food chains. Just let your stomach and your pocketbook be your guide.

Two spots that many vacationers overlook—and, thus, miss some dining treats—are several fine restaurants in the city of Panama City, eastward across Hathaway Bridge from the resort communities, and westward toward a community called Seagrove. For some reason not completely clear, a number of truly outstanding upscale eating spots have sprung up among the coastal scrub. Some are quite pricey, but rarely do they disappoint the most discriminating palate.

What to do before and after the dive?

Well, after you see the Museum of Man in the Sea, just name it.

The museum is managed by the Panama City Marine Institute—the same outfit responsible for developing many of the dive spots that you will enjoy. It houses relics from the first days of scuba diving and underwater exploration.

There is treasure recovered from shipwrecks, and historical displays depicting man's fascination with the underwater world dating back to 1500. The museum is open daily from 9 a.m. to 5 p.m. It is on Back Beach Road, about a quarter mile west of Florida 79.

Then pick your pleasure. Amusement parks, go-cart racing, wave runners, sailing, moonlight dinner cruises, night clubbing, beachside amusement parks, a country music hall, sun bathing, golf, tennis...this could go on forever, but you get the idea.

For more information on the Panama City area, write or call:

Panama City Beaches Chamber of Commerce
P.O. Box 9348
Panama City Beach, FL 32407
1-800-PCBEACH
(904)235-1159

Panama City Diving

There are nine dive shops in the Panama City area, some being separate stores with common ownership.

The shops are well-developed, with most offering air, equipment sales, rental and repair and dive charters.

Following is a list of the dive shops, their addresses and phone numbers:

Captain Black's Dive Shop
at St. Andrews State Park
Panama City Beach, FL
(904)233-0504
Diver's Den
4720 E. Business Hwy. 98
Parker, FL
(904)871-6375

(Diver's Den beach store)
3804 Thomas Drive
Panama City Beach, FL 32408
(904)234-8717
Emerald Coast Diver's Den
6222 E. Highway 98
Panama City, FL 32404
(904)871-2876

(Emerald Coast Diver's Den city marina location)
1 Harrison Ave.
Panama City, FL 32404
(904)769-6621

Holiday Scuba Center
at Sun Harbor Marina
P.O. Box 4645
Panama City, FL 32401-4645
(904)785-8436

Hydrospace Dive Shop
6422 West Highway 98
Panama City Beach, FL
(904)234-3063
1-800-874-3483
(904)233-9657 (fax)

(Hydrospace shop at Treasure Ship marina area)
3605-A Thomas Drive
Panama City Beach, FL
(904)234-9463

Panama City Dive Center
4823 Thomas Drive
Panama City, FL 32408
(904)235-3390
1-800-832-DIVE
(904)233-0624 (fax)

The hardware store offering some dive equipment is C&G Sporting Goods, 137 Harrison Ave., Panama City, FL. It does not offer air fills.

While most shops provide frequent dive trips—several daily during the warm months—it still is advisable to check on availability ahead of time and reserve a space.

Trips do fill up quickly.

Dive charter captains are experienced and can provide divers efficient, enjoyable trips. They know how to take the hassle out of a trip, and make sure that attention is focused on the diver having a good time.

Two-tank dives typically range in cost from $35 to $45 per person, and range upward to $60 or more per person for trips to distant offshore locations.

Some experienced boaters choose to dive from their own boats. Make sure you know what you are doing. While the gulf is considered a calm sea, it can be unforgiving. Just count the number of shipwrecks in the listing that follows.

There are public launch ramps on the west side of Grand Lagoon, although some in recent years have fallen into disrepair. Check them carefully before backing your trailer in.

Other public ramps are at St. Andrews State Park on Grand Lagoon and on St. Andrews Bay at the west end of Hathaway Bridge.

There are two exits from the bay to the gulf. The primary and by far the most navigable is the ship channel, which separates the mainland from Shell Island. It is straight, deep and well marked by buoys. Watch for traffic. Panama City is a deep-water port and the channel is used by commercial and Navy ships, not to mention the many private and commercial sport, fishing and dive boats.

The channel is flanked by rock jetties. The rocks extend underwater. Take care not to whang up your propeller on them. It will ruin your day.

At the other end of Shell Island is a relatively shallow, narrow, crooked channel that opens to the gulf. Be careful. Depths can jump from 10 feet to 10 inches in an instant. It is a pretty place to visit, but be prepared to navigate some shallows.

Following is a listing and brief description of Panama City's favorite dive spots.

Bay Dives/St. Andrews Bay

Even with its commercial shipping this is one of the most pollution-free bays along the northern gulf. Thus the bay offers good visibility during most of the year, except after harsh weather, and best on an incoming or slack high tide.

Grass flats
Located behind Shell Island, these broad grass-covered flats are interspersed with expanses of white sand. Hundreds of species of sea life are hatched in this estuary each year. The flats, which begin at the shore and extend to depths of 15 to 20 feet, also are home for a population of bay scallops which divers (and waders) gather in season. This is a great snorkeling spot where divers can find shells, starfish, sea horses, stone and blue crabs and a variety of fish and rays. Porpoise cavort along the deeper edges of the flats, and will come right alongside a diver.

Life Boats
Grouper, flounder, occasional triggerfish, some tropicals and shells are found around this group of lifeboats that were chained together and sunk behind Shell Island. The steel-hull boats, each roughly 30-feet long, lie in 28 feet of water. They came from old liberty ships that were scrapped some years back. They are on soft bottom that is easily stirred, causing visibility problems. Visibility normally ranges from five to about 20 feet.

Landmark Apartments Site
Just offshore from the Landmark Apartments are the remains of

DIVE

NORTH FLORIDA'S BEST DIVING

Gulf Coast's Largest & Most Experienced Dive Service

Daily Wreck & Reef Dives

Fast Customized Dive Boats

Dive The Worlds Most Beautiful Beaches

1-800-874-3483

HYDROSPACE

DIVE SHOP.™

6422 West Highway 98
Panama City Beach, FL
(904)234-3063

3605 A. Thomas Drive
Panama City Beach, FL
(904) 234-9463

an old ice house. A variety of tropicals call the spot home. Depth is under 20 feet.

Tar Barge

In 16 to 18 feet of water, this old barge sits at the broad mouth of Spanish Shanty Cove. The 150-foot barge is showing its age with holes all in it, many from careless boaters hanging their anchors into it. The barge holds a nice sheepshead, flounder and grouper population, and other sea life such as gray snappers and speckled trout (spotted weakfish) are seen from time to time. Shells, sea urchins and sand dollars are all about. Visibility ranges to about 15 feet on an average day.

Bay Dumpsters

12 garbage dumpsters were sunk behind Shell Island, fairly near the ship channel, which provides clearer water and greater visibility than most other bay sites. They are in approximately 15 feet of water. The dumpsters hold stone crabs, shells, tropicals and flounder.

Shore Dives

Jetties

The jetties flanking the ship channel—one on Shell Island, the other on the mainland at St. Andrews State Park form one of the finest shore dives in the northern gulf. These man-made stone jetties attract a variety of sea life, from stone crabs to octopi, mullet, triggerfish, plentiful tropicals, crustaceans, flounder, rays, small grouper, grunts, croakers, whiting and a colorful mixture of redfish, jacks, mackerel, ladyfish, hardtails and other fish that school in and out of the rocks season by season. At certain times, specks, bluefish and redfish are plentiful around the jetties. Visibility can range from poor to more than 50 feet, depending on tides. The best time to dive the jetties is on an incoming tide or at slack high tide for two reasons. That is when water is clearest, and if you like to drift along with the tide looking at the sights, the tide will be pulling you into the bay instead of out to sea. It is illegal to spearfish or gather marine souvenirs.

Surf

Diving along Panama City's beaches can be a discouraging

exercise for a visiting diver. It looks like so many miles of underwater Sahara—acre upon acre of rippled sand without barrier or reef. Frankly, the surf of the northern gulf is basically soft flat sand with a couple of rolls of sand bars as you look seaward. Except during rough seas, the surf is generally clear and currents are light. For the novice snorkeler, it can provide hours of fun. Sea shells can be found on the sea side of the sand bars and in the trough between them. And, an amazing number of fish will be seen. Croaker, grunts, pinfish, pompano, hardtails and whiting school along the shore in large numbers. Occasional flounder, rays and crabs venture by. Sometimes divers will see ladyfish, redfish, mackerel, speckled trout and mullet. Flags indicating surf conditions—roughness of seas and strength of currents—are flown at a number of locations along the beach. Check before diving. While the northern gulf generally is a gentle and calm sea, it does have its strong and violent moments.

Open Gulf

Diving opportunities in the open Gulf of Mexico are what draw divers to this region. Shipwrecks can be found in water ranging from 20 to 40 feet and deeper, while most reefs will be in at least 60 feet of water, and usually in deeper water.

Except during stormy weather (which you won't be able to make a dive trip anyway) expect visibility of 40 to near 100 feet.

Open gulf trips typically are two-tank dives and dive boat runs can range from a half hour to near two hours, depending on the area that you have arranged to dive. The longer trips cost more and usually have to be arranged in advance.

There are three types of popular dives—wrecks, artificial reefs and natural reefs. While Panama City has an abundance of each, it is best known for its shipwreck diving.

Wrecks

Shipwrecks are dramatic dives. Most boast huge populations of sea life and because of that spearfishing and photography are popular. Massive schools of baitfish, so huge that they look like moving walls that block out the sun, swarm around many of the wrecks.

Shells and sand dollars gather around wrecks. Fish include all open gulf species. Commonly seen are flounder, jacks, snapper, triggerfish, barracuda, grunts, several species of tropicals, grouper, spadefish, with pelagic species torpedoing their way in and out.

Empire Mica

Many divers throughout the Southeast consider this wreck the best of them all. The tanker was torpedoed by a German submarine in 1942 just southeast of Cape San Blas, south of Panama City. The 465-foot ship lies in about 100 feet of water. Shell collecting, spear fishing and artifact hunting are considered excellent. Divers can see the two torpedo holes in the ship's hull and her 18-foot spare propeller. The main propeller was removed by divers about a decade ago, and now is on display outside Captain Anderson's Restaurant at Grand Lagoon. 14023.5/46489.6

Gray Ghost

A 105-foot Navy tug was intentionally sunk in 105 feet of water in 1978, due west of the jetties. The tug lies on its side near some live bottom and growth has accumulated rapidly. About 20 miles from the pass, but because if its dramatic profile still a favorite of area divers. 13891.1/46991.7

Leroy

Built in the 1800s, the 129-foot Leroy sank in the 1920s 20 miles south of Panama City in 120 feet of water. The boiler, some timbers and littered debris are about all that remain. The ship started out as a revenue cutter, but later was converted to a tug boat by a Pensacola company. She was on her way to Tampa in 1926 when she sprang a leak in rough water and sank. 13927.3/46903.9

Liberty Ship

A scuttled 441-foot-long, 57-foot-wide liberty ship was sunk off Panama City in 1977 in 74 feet of water. It is 7.5 miles south southwest of the pass. The ship was cut to the waterline before being sent down. Still, the wreck rises 20 feet from the bottom. Additional material has been sunk both inside and outside the hull through the years to prompt growth and accumulation of sea life. The ship originally was the Benjamin H. Grierson, built by the Oregon Ship Building Corp. in Portland. 14065.1/46918.6

Simpson

This 93-foot tug sank in the late 1920s about a half mile outside the old St. Andrews Bay pass at the south end of Shell Island. She lies in about 20 feet of water. It is the shallowest open gulf wreck in the Panama City area. The Simpson also was a Pensacola-based tug, and was attempting to free a grounded fishing boat in rough weather when she capsized and the crew had to abandon ship. The crew spent the night on Shell Island and by the next morning the ship was on the bottom. The ship's smokestack can be seen just below the surface on calm days. 14121.5/46942.5

Tarpon

This 160-foot ship was a familiar sight along the Florida gulf coast during its developmental days. It was a strategic lifeline, bringing news, supplies and, sometimes, passengers to areas where roads were few and usually poor. The ship, built in 1887, went down in late summer, 1937, in heavy seas. The Tarpon lies in approximately

Baitfish, an angel fish, grunts and vermilion snapper crowd around a cranny in the Chickasaw wreck off Panama City
Photo courtesy of Davy Jones Locker, Mobile, Ala.

90 feet of water, 9.5 miles west of the pass. Lying on hard bottom the wreck offers a wealth of sea life, including both game and tropical fish. Old beer bottles, part of the Tarpon's cargo when she went down, are among the artifacts that divers regularly bring up from the wreck. 13979.6/47001.9

Commander

Only 60 feet long and 15 feet wide, the Commander sits on sand bottom. Since it is intact and with a number of portholes, it seems to be attracting a large amount of sea life. The boat lies in 90 to 100 feet of water 15 miles west of the pass. 13967.8/46982.5

USS Strength

This Navy tender to a minesweeping fleet was purposefully sunk in 1987 for naval exercises. Only 5.5 miles south southwest from the pass, the ship lies in 72 feet of water. Because of the nearness to port and the fact that the Strength's deck lies only 40 feet beneath the surface, this is one of Panama City's favorite dives. The strength is more than 180 feet long and 33 feet wide. 14076.7/46943.9

Chippewa

A 225-foot long ocean going tug, the Chippewa lies on an even keel on a level white sand bottom. About 11 miles south southwest— or straight out the pass—the out the pass. It has been there for a number of years and is deteriorating on the ends. 14065.7/46981.0

Chickasaw

The approximately 100-foot-long steel-hull tug sank in the late 1970s in 72 feet of water, straight out the pass and within a half mile of the sea buoy--about three miles from the pass. The tug was built in Pensacola in the early 1900s and was used to help build the Panama City jetties before being retired after World War II.

Barges

Barges may not evoke the same romantic images as sunken ships, but do not underestimate their value as an interesting dive. They attract a variety of sea life--shells, sand dollars and lots of tropical, bait and game fish.

And no area has done a better job of developing dive sites with barges than has Panama City.

N.W. FLORIDA

DIVING
WRECKS · REEFS · SPRINGS

- Largest Charter Fleat

- Warm / Clear Waters

- Professional / Friendly Service

- Group Rates Available

 # Panama City Dive Center

Nitrox Facility

Scuba Pro   Sherwood   Oceanic   JBL

904-235-3390
**4823 Thomas Dr.
(on the Beach)
Panama City Beach, Florida**

1-800-832-DIVE

More than a dozen barges lie in Panama City waters from less than 40 to more than 100 feet. The deeper the water, the more reliable is visibility.

Holland barge is in 65 feet of water, almost directly out the pass. It has been there for a number of years and is deteriorating on the ends.

Joe Smith barge lies in about 70 feet of water and sea life has increased around the barge thanks to the aid of several loads of artificial reef material being dumped in the area. 14066.9/46976.0

P.C. barge lies in 50 feet of water off the Long Beach Resort area of Panama City Beach. The barge has been there for a number of years and also has had additional loads of artificial reef material dumped around it. 14067.3/47018.3

Twin barges are two barges about 300 yards apart in just over 70 feet of water. One lies inshore of the other; thus they are known as the Inshore Twin and the Offshore Twin. Going out to the sea buoy these two barges lie roughly on a 90 degree left turn. It is perhaps three to four miles off the pass. Inshore: 14069.0/46968.0. Offshore: 14067.7/46967.0

Blown barge got its name from the manner in which it was sent to the bottom. As it turned out the size of the charge sent chunks of barge over a fairly wide area of bottom, about 70 feet down. The barge is on a line just right of the pass and about seven or eight miles out. Several loads of artificial reef material have been added to help attract sea life. 14053.2/46992.6

Davis barge is in 55 feet of water off the east end of Shell Island, which makes it a longer run than many of the other barges. It is perhaps less than three miles from shore, making a good dive opportunity on days when a strong wind is blowing from the north or east. 14116.0/46916.4

Deep barge lies in about 90 feet of water, just west of the Stage I Navy tower site. It is a popular second dive for those diving the tower wreckage or some of the live bottom in the same area. Spear fishing is considered very good. 13979.9/46962.9

PCMI barge gets its name from the Panama City Marine Institute which spends a great deal of time, effort and money developing havens of sea life to benefit fishermen and divers. This barge is in about 65 feet of water, just west of the Stage II Navy tower wreckage. The 115-foot barge has some hard bottom around it which enhances development of sea life. 14043.8/47001.6

B&B barge is a shallow dive, about 30 feet. It is just offshore of Shell Island, situated about half way between the ship channel and the old pass. 14087.3/46970.7

Murphy's barge lies in 50 feet of water about a mile beyond the B&B barge and is broken up. A lot of metal artificial reef material has been added to the site, which is reported to hold good sea life, including legal-length grouper.

Navy trash pile barge was sunk near an artificial reef made of culverts. This barge lies in the Navy Trash Pile area in 62 feet of water. It is reported to hold a great deal of sea.

Artificial Reefs

Some of the barges in the previous section are the centerpieces of larger artificial reef systems, which makes them even more heavily populated with sea life.

These artificial sites can consist of anything that has a hard surface. Fishermen and divers have used everything from PVC pipe to car bodies to bridge rubble. The key is to put down something that plant life will attach to.

Once the plant life begins to grow, minnows come to nibble. Larger fish come to nibble the minnows.

Artificial reefs change with age, particular those made of metal that rust away. However, once an artificial reef has established itself, fishermen and divers usually nourish it by adding new material to enlarge the area and replace those items that rusted away.

DRIVE A LITTLE, SAVE A LOT!

EMERALD COAST DIVER'S DEN
PANAMA CITY, FLORIDA

DACOR • SEAQUEST • MARES • PARKWAY • JBL • WENOKA • IKELITE SSA • DEEPSEE • ORCA

EMERALD COAST
D I V E R ' S   D E N

DACOR

1 Harrison Ave.
Panama City, FL
769-6621

6222 E. Hwy 98
Panama City, FL
871-2876

Navy Towers wreckage

Until the mid-1980s the U.S. Navy maintained two towers off Panama City. Each looked similar to an oil drilling platform, sitting atop steel pilings that extended from the gulf floor to above the surface. The members criss-crossed with supporting and stabilizing beams, all attracting crustaceans and a multitude of sea life.

The tower nearest shore— three miles off and to the north of the pass—was known as Stage II. It sat in 55 feet of water. The second tower was about 12 miles straight out the pass in 105 feet of water.

Both towers were abandoned and dropped into the sea in the 1980s. Although Panama City lost two of its most famous landmarks—or, perhaps, seamarks—it did not lose them as dive spots.

Massive schools of baitfish swarm around the sites, along with a variety of reef fish and pelagic species in season. Both spots usually offer good visibility, with the more distant tower superior to the inshore tower site. In addition, the offshore tower usually boasts much larger fish.

The inshore tower has several artificial reefs around it, including a T-33 Navy trainer jet that the government donated. Stage I: 13980.0/46957.9. Stage II: 14068.8/46997.8

Warsaw Site

Old tires, scrap concrete, old trucks, bridge spans, bridge rubble and a bus lie about seven miles southwest of the pass in 70 feet of water. This is a large area, with sea life concentrating around the structure. 14036.8/46977.2

Midway

In about 75 feet of water and half way between the jetties and the liberty ship wreck. This large area includes a variety of material, highlighted by a helicopter body, a pontoon and two 60-foot railroad cars, which are reported to be deteriorating rapidly. This area usually is very good for shells. 14072.6/46949.6

Fontainebleu site

Also in about 75 feet of water, this reef northwest of the jetties gets its name by being directly offshore from a resort of the same name. The site includes bridge rubble and spans, a plane, boxcars and other material. The reef has been in place for some time, has some hard bottom nearby and usually holds a good population of sea life. 14019.8/47028.2

Navy Trash Pile

This large area lies about three miles off Shell Island and has been used as a Navy dumping ground for many years. It contains a little of everything—from old chains to airplane parts to all sorts of metal containers. The entire area holds fish well. 14079.4/46973.5

Loss Pontoon

This large Navy pontoon once was used to lift salvageable items from the sea floor. When surplus, the Panama City Marine Institute sank the 80-ton vessel in 60 feet of water three miles off Shell Island. It is 15 feet in diameter and 40 feet long. 14078.5/46973.8

Quonset Hut

This large metal cylinder got its name because divers think it looks like an example of the semi-circular military training housing of the same name. It lies in almost 90 feet of water 10 miles. The cylinder is over 40 feet long and 30 feet across. A top spearfishing spot. 14011.0/46697.1

Navy Tanks

These two metal cylinders, six feet across and 25 feet long lie in 70 feet of water. Some say the cylinders were intended to be part of the Navy Trash Pile, but wound up some distance away. Other artificial reef material has been added through the years. 14078.0/46973.7

The original
Diver's Den

3804 Thomas Drive
Panama City Beach
Florida
(904) 234-8717

Sales * Service
Instruction * Charters

Best quality
Best value
For all your diving needs

P.C. Barge Airplane

This airplane, an Air Force drone, lies near the P.C. barge to enhance the site as an artificial reef system. 14042.5/47002.4

Hathaway Bridge Rubble

In the late 1980s the old Hathaway Bridge spanning St. Andrews Bay was dismantled and placed offshore in 19 locations to form fishing and diving spots. Participating in the project were the Florida Department of Transportation and Panama City Marine Institute. The sites range in depth from just over 40 to 125 feet deep. The closest is about two miles offshore, while the greatest distance is 15 miles. The rubble consisted of roadbed decks and iron superstructure. The superstructure spans are more than 165-feet long and rise more than 35 feet off the bottom. Deck spans are much smaller so they were dumped in groups of three and four. They are just under 50 feet long and stand about six feet off the bottom. Locations are:

13949.8/46950.0	13952.7/46969.6
13953.8/46955.8	13955.4/46961.0
13995.2/46923.3	13997.9/46915.8
14002.1/46920.1	14002.4/46914.3
14003.8/46970.3	14019.3/47031.1
14020.1/47022.8	14025.2/47030.3
14031.8/46977.0	14037.2/46977.4
14068.8/46949.0	14070.6/46953.1
14074.5/46946.5	14085.4/46974.0

Boxcars

A number of boxcars were dumped in 18 different groups several years ago. Some were dumped in the vicinity of other rubble to improve the quality of existing artificial reefs, while others were formed as the basis for new reefs. The barges are in water from 45 to 110 feet. Reports are that the near-shore barges are deteriorating rapidly, but that the deeper barges are holding up well. Each site holds the same type of sea life as other artificial reefs. Sites include:

14011.5/46925.5	14019.8/47028.2
14067.4/47018.3	14072.4/46949.6
14076.5/46944.3	

Highway 331 Rubble

After a barge hit and damaged a bridge spanning the eastern end of Choctawhatchee Bay, arrangements were made for the bridge segments that had to be replaced to be used for artificial reef building. The rubble was placed in seven different locations of 20 to 30 spans each only recently, and reports are that sea life is gathering quickly. Each span is about 25 by 35 feet and stands about five feet tall. Since they were dumped in groups, the piles of rubble stand 15 to 20 feet off the bottom. Mostly concrete, this rubble will make permanent reef locations and only get better with age. Sites include:

14033.8/46972.4	14052.4/46992.5
14066.9/46976.1	14067.4/47018.4
14072.3/46951.5	14072.3/46072.3
14074.5/46950.0	14080.2/46977.8

Natural Reefs

These reefs are typical of those found throughout the northern gulf—limestone ledges ranging from but a few inches to a number of feet high.

Some are long straight ledges, while others have holes and curves. Others are patch reefs and include fans and sponges. The reefs begin in about 50 or 60 feet of water and extend into depths of more than 100 feet.

Because of their depths and because northern gulf waters cool significantly in winter, the coral on these reefs does not grow to the luxurious size of that of the Florida Keys. Even so soft and small hard coral does grow in these reefs.

All are havens for tropical sea life, shells, anemones and animals ranging from the shovelnose lobster to angel fish to many reef fish, eels, octopi, sharks and turtles.

Warsaw Hole

This probably is Panama City's best known and one of its closest reefs. It is easy to find and quick to get to. It lies about seven or eight miles directly out the pass. It is a semi-circular reef in 80 to 90 feet of water. The ledge rises to six feet and is covered with sea flora. Game fish come and go, but tropicals and shells can always be found. 14033.7/46969.2

Phillips Inlet Reefs

This area about 15 to 19 miles west of the pass is covered with reefs from less than 60 to just over 100 feet. Sandstone and limestone ledges teem with lobster and game fish. Large basket sponges and other sea life make for great underwater photography. The reef area spreads southward like a fan from Phillips Inlet (marked by Pinnacle Port condominium). The series of reefs range for miles with ledges ranging upward to eight feet. Some of the well-known reefs in the area and their depths are Nine-Fathom Hole (54), Horseshoe Reef (65), Peppertree (70), Kelley Reef (70), Quartermile Reef (74), Anchorless Reef (74), Tarpon Reef (90), Grey Reefs (95), Barbers Reef (102), Center Reef (102), Round Rock Reef (102) and Trinity Reefs (93).

Northwest of Stage I

An area of low patch reef ledges run in a southeast to northwest line from near the Stage I site. These ledges long have been regularly worked by party boats and, to some extent, by charter boats as well. These reefs hold good populations of vermilion snapper, triggerfish, white snapper and grouper—staples of the party boat trade. Divers too frequent the area, although they more frequently opt for the higher ledge reefs of Phillips Inlet. Still, these patch reefs teem with sea life and have colorful and luxurious plant life growing on and around them.

South of Stage I

There are a series of four- to six-foot breaks in 115 feet of water south of the Stage I site. These breaks hold good populations of snapper and grouper and are favorite spots for spearfishing as well as rod-and-reel fishing. They also have all the other types of sea life common to northern gulf reef areas.

Schools of sardines swarm over Destin bridge rubble
Photo Courtesy of Captain J's Dive Shop, Destin

Destin/Fort Walton Beach

The Area

These two cities are grouped in a single chapter, but it is important to know that the dive boats and the channel from the harbor to the Gulf of Mexico are at Destin. Fort Walton Beach is only minutes west on U.S. 98, and is included in the chapter because it is home for several dive shops and major entertainment, dining and lodging accommodations.

Heading westward from Panama City, East Pass at Destin is the next available opening to the gulf from a protected harbor.

Thirty years ago, the two communities was separated by 50 miles of lonesome pine scrub and palmettos. Like most places, however, the years have brought growth and the two resort areas are slowly but surely growing closer together.

The communities of Blue Mountain Beach, Santa Rosa Beach, Seaside, Seagrove and Grayton Beach are worth excursions off the main road. Carved out of the scrub are model communities of beach homes, luxurious condominiums, fine restaurants and eclectic shops. As you draw nearer Destin you begin to see not only the typical array of beach shops, but also dramatic resort communities.

Destin has an upscale feeling, starting with the shining high-rise condos that dot the shoreline.

It was not always that way. Destin was established as a tiny fishing village on a bluff overlooking a protected harbor at the mouth of Choctawhatchee Bay. The harbor actually once was the channel from the bay to the gulf. But after a storm closed the original pass, Destin residents dug the present channel.

The harbor is home to what some say is Florida's largest sport fishing fleet. The reason for Destin's founding, gathering of the large fishing fleet and the community's slogan, "Luckiest Fishing Village in the World" are the multitude of reefs that spread seaward in every direction from the mouth of East Pass. The first ones can be found less than two miles out and extend outward to the great cliffs of the DeSoto Canyon.

In these rocky outcroppings live sea life of every description, including some species normally found only hundreds of miles to the south. Speculation is that these out-of-place species find their way to Destin waters by riding the Gulf Stream's loop current that circles up Mexico's east coast, past the northern gulf and then back down the Florida west coast. Nowhere closer to land does this open ocean stream flow than the shores of Destin.

But back to shore.

It has been in just the past 30 years that Fort Walton Beach has grown from a small village on Santa Rosa Sound to a city of more than 20,000. With several military bases surrounding the city, it has a definite military air.

Fort Walton Beach boasts a number of fine restaurants, two outlet shopping malls, an old business district that has developed into a fine tourist shopping area.

There are more than 8,000 accommodations, with price ranges to fit a variety of budgets.

In addition to water sports, Fort Walton Beach offers 11 golf courses, tennis courts, marinas, an Indian Temple Mound and museum, a marine aquarium complex—the Gulfarium, parasailing, water slides, miniature golf courses, bumper boats, go-cart tracks, a military air museum and shopping galore.

A calendar of events seems to sport more events, festivals, fishing tournaments and shows than there are days in the year. Something always is going on. No diver will want for something to do during shore time. The problem will be picking and choosing.

Fort Walton Beach and Destin are connected by a six-mile stretch of U.S. 98 surrounded by brilliant high white dunes and flanked on the north by Choctawhatchee Bay and on the south by the Gulf of Mexico.

A breathtaking sight is the bay and gulf from the tall bridge spanning East Pass. At high tide, the clear channel waters are a variety of hues that change with the channel's depth. The blue waters of the gulf and bay stretch away to either side, and gleaming condos stretch into the distance.

Once over the bridge heading east, the harbor is to the immediate south and it is lined with docks for three miles or so. A favorite pastime is to wander the docks in the late afternoon when the fishing and dive boats are coming in. It is easy to ooh and aah over the day's catch as deck hands pile the catch on the dock for cleaning.

While fishing still remains the centerpiece of Destin activity, it is a long way from being the only thing going on.

There is a water park, children's park including bumper boats and cars and go-carts, sailing, jet skis and a number of fine golf courses, tennis courts, clubs and restaurants.

There is a good division of activities for both adults and children.

Where to Stay

With more than 8,000 rooms in the area, lodging seems plentiful, but can sell out on summer weekends and around holidays.

Accommodations range from the luxurious high-rise gulf front condos to secluded bed and breakfast inns to mom and pop motels. Some complexes have their own golf and tennis complexes, while others are merely overnight rooms for rent.

This is one resort where the harbor is as in demand as a location as is the gulf itself, and moreso for those who bring their own boat and want to dock outside their door.

Several campgrounds are available in the Destin area, at least one with gulf front. Unfortunately there are no camping opportunities on the harbor. There is a nice bay front campground near Niceville, named Rocky Bayou, about eight miles across the bay and north of the pass. While it does not have formal dock facilities, there are places where a boat can be tied off for overnight stays.

Grayton Beach State Park between Destin and Panama City also offers camping in a beach and dune lake setting.

Destin Chamber of Commerce publishes a guidebook with

telephone numbers and addresses of area properties. The chamber's number is (904)837-6241.

So what's to eat?

Likewise, diners can find upscale restaurants offering exquisite cuisine (and some as exquisite prices, although not necessarily overpriced for what one gets), while there are others catering to families and are more budget minded. Seafood, of course, is king here, with a number of restaurants offering locally-developed recipes for amberjack, dolphin, triggerfish, grouper, snapper and other local species.

Bring in your own catch and several restaurants will prepare it for you.

Most restaurants are concentrated on U.S. 98, the main drag through Destin. In season, it indeed is a drag, laden with vacationers. There are a number of fine restaurants right along the 4-lane, with signs directing visitors to other restaurants just down the bluff to the harbor's edge.

A new U.S. 98 bypasses the beach for several miles on the east end of Destin. Some restaurants have sprung up along the new roadway. But don't forget to slip over to the old 98, now a local access beach road. It also is home to a number of great restaurants.

Lastly, that stretch of beach around Santa Rosa, Grayton Beach, Seaside and Seagrove shouldn't be overlooked. Some of the region's finest restaurants call it home.

There are, of course, the normal fast food spots and chain restaurants.

When you're not diving

In addition to the golf, tennis, water park, go-carts and other commercial entertainment, Grayton Beach State Park is a nice quick visit as is nearby Eden State Gardens, 30 miles east of Destin. The site includes the restored Eden mansion from the 1800s.

The docks themselves are interesting places to stroll, visit and hang out. They are havens for salty characters, fish tales, oyster and gumbo bars, and a glimpse of the fishes that you will see on your dive trips. The docks are in segments, each run by an individual or group, but still it is fairly easy to transition from one to the next for a walking tour of a couple miles. There are several places to stop along the way for raw oysters, a seafood snack and something cold to drink.

The Gulfarium at Fort Walton Beach is a fine salt-water aquarium with reef and trained porpoise exhibits. It has been there many years and was putting on first class programs long before the national aquarium craze of the past several years.

Sailboat, powerboat and cruise rentals are available for open gulf and harbor tours.

Then there is fishing. After all, that *is* why Destin is here. There is bay fishing, surf fishing, jetty fishing, pier fishing, trolling and bottom fishing. It can be cheap and easy, or rugged and expensive.

Light tackle can be used for surf, jetty and some pier fishing. Bait is cheap, or can be, and several species from these areas make fine table fare. Check with local tackle shops to see what is biting. Check also for local limits, seasons and whether you need a license.

Boat fishing comes in two broad types—party boats and charter boats. Party boats are larger and fishermen buy tickets that provide them with a rod and reel, bait, ice and a reserved spot at the rail from which to bottom fish. The captain takes them to artificial or natural reef areas where they catch bottom fish for a designated period of time. Visitors can locate party boats offering half, three-quarter and full-day trips.

Charter boats generally are smaller, faster, can fish smaller spots and allow the fisherman some more control over the type fishing that is done. However, don't take this to extreme. The best bet is to take the captain's advice on what to fish for. He knows what's biting. However, a charter boat can vary a trip to allow trolling, bottom fishing, light-line fishing and other custom styles of fishing. The charter fisherman also will be more effective going after specific types of fish. Of course, charter boats generally cost more per person for a day of fishing.

For more information on the Destin and Fort Walton Beach areas, write or call:

Greater Fort Walton Beach Chamber of Commerce
P.O. Box 640
Fort Walton Beach, FL 32549
(904)244-8191

Destin Chamber of Commerce
P.O. Box 8
1021 Highway 98 East
Destin, FL 32540
(904)837-6241

Destin/Fort Walton Beach Diving

There are six dive shops serving this area, plus a number of charter boats offering trips and one snorkeling-only service.

The shops are well equipped, offering air, equipment sales, rental and repair and charters.

Following is a list of the dive shops, their addresses and phone numbers:

Aquanaut Scuba Center, Inc.
24 Highway 98
P.O. Box 651
Destin, FL 32541
(904)837-0359

Captain J's Dive Shop
301 Highway 98 East
Destin, FL 32541
(904)654-5300 or (904)654-1616
1-800-677-DIVE

Fantasea Scuba
#1 Highway 98 East
P.O. Box 5498
Destin, FL 32540
(904)837-0732 or (904)837-6943
1-800-326-2732

Scuba Experience
234 SE Miracle Strip Parkway
Fort Walton Beach, FL 32548
(904)244-WETT

ScubaTech
5371 Highway 98 East
Destin, FL 32541
(904)837-1933

ScubaTech (harbor location)
312 Highway 98 East
Destin, FL 32541
(904)837-2822

The Scuba Shop
348 Miracle Strip Parkway, #19
Fort Walton Beach, FL 32548
(904)243-1600

The snorkeling-only location is Kokomo Motel & Marina, 500 Highway 98, Destin, FL 32541. Phone is (904)837-9029 or (904)837-6171.

The shops provide frequent dive trips—several daily during the warm months—it still is advisable to check on availability ahead of time and reserve a space.

Trips fill up quickly.

Dive charter captains are experienced, know how to provide safe, efficient and interesting trips. Two tank dives generally cost about $40, with the diver supplying all equipment. Dive costs can range to more than $60 per person for specialized dives or trips to distant locations.

Experienced boaters can dive from their own boats, but this is not advised for the boater inexperienced in salt-water, open-sea navigation for several reasons:

1. East Pass has a shallow opening where waves build up quickly when wind picks up. A boater inexperienced with this type wave pattern or who has ventured out the pass in calm weather only to find the waves upon his return can get in trouble in a hurry.

2. While there are lots of reefs and wrecks off Destin, if you do not have Loran numbers you can spend many gallons of gas motoring around with just a depth finder. If you don't have a depth finder or loran—and ship-to-shore radio—you don't need to be out there.

3. Getting on top of reefs, staying there, having an experienced person topside, keeping track of surface intervals and all that sort of stuff should not be left to the casual boater.

But if you can handle it all, there are several public ramps around the harbor, in the vicinity of marinas.

Once you clear East Pass the gulf is obstruction free, quickly descending to a depth of 40 or 50 feet and, with gentle hills and valleys, generally descends to greater depths as you go further from shore.

Bay Dives

Choctawhatchee Bay is not a terribly polluted bay, but generally lacks sufficient visibility for diving. Mostly it is a dishpan-type bay with a flat bottom about 30 feet down, tapering upward around the edges. Sand bars jut out into the bay from points. Be careful. You can go from 30 to 3 feet in nothing flat. Channels are well marked. Pay attention.

Bay Cones

A reef of cones and mailboxes and other rubble lies in 25 to 30 feet of water about a mile inside the mouth of the bay. The cones are in three groups of three. Each cone is 10 to 12 feet in diameter and eight feet high. The area holds spadefish, tropicals and small grouper. Visibility on good days can range to near 30 feet.

Shrimp Boat

Some local divers say they have dove this spot, while others profess to only hearing about it. Those who have been there say that the boat lies in 30 to 35 feet of water and holds flounder, small grouper, some vermilion and white snapper and stone crabs.

Sand Bar and Grass Flats

At the mouth of Choctawhatchee Bay, just north of the Destin bridge is a huge sand bar that has become a popular anchorage and snorkeling spot. It is best snorkeled at slack high tide. Frankly tides can be a bit heavy at times and there isn't much sea life on the bar except for an occasional blue crab scuttling along. The bar seems to be much more a socializing location for boaters and snorkelers than a place to see a variety of sea life.

North of the bar and across the channel are grass flats that hold tropicals and crabs. They also need to be visited during high tide.

Destin Bridge

The abutments and piers of the bridge spanning East Pass offers a varied dive that can range from snorkeling the shallows of the western half (where most diver's begin this dive) to depths of more than 40 feet at the bottom of the channel. Currents here can be treacherous, so diving the channel should be attempted only at high tide. Divers can expect to see crabs, tropicals, game fish, shells, occasional schools of squid and baitfish. There is a lot of boat traffic in the area so display your dive flag prominently. The parking area at the west end of the bridge allows divers to drive within yards of the water and the bottom slopes downward for easy entry. Spearfishing is illegal.

East Pass Jetties

Stone jetties flank the east and west sides of East Pass. The west-side jetties can be entered from the gulf-side shore and divers can swim their length. Depths range from shore to 10 or 15 feet until near the southernmost tip they drop to a hole of 30 feet or better.

The channel side is much shallower, with a broad sand bar extending for many yards toward the channel. It also is a good snorkeling location, but the sand bar makes getting there tricky for boaters.

On the east side the jetty extends only half way down the pass, making a left turn where sand has built up to form a comfortable

Discover *Fantasea* **SCUBA** **Destin**

SPEND YOUR VACATION
DIVING NOT *DRIVING*

• Snorkel and scuba gear rentals
• Hotel/dive packages available
• Underwater videos available
• NACD Cave Diving Facility
• Student referrals

• Family snorkeling tours
• Daily reef trips on the 45 ft. Fantasea and new 31 ft. Extasea
• Northwest Florida's oldest **PADI** 5-star training facility and Instructor Development Center

FANTASEA SCUBA HEADQUARTERS
#1 Miracle Strip Pkwy.
P.O. Box 5498 • Destin, FL 32540
At the Foot of the Destin Bridge
(904) 837-0732   (904) 837-6943
FAX (904) 837-7392   (800) 326-2732

swimming beach. This is where divers usually enter the water to dive the rock area. This area is considered among the area's best shore dives. Young snorkelers can spend hours in the two- to four-foot shallows peering at the tropicals, baitfish and occasional gray snapper darting in and out of the rocks. Sometimes shells and sand dollars wash in. The jetty extends outward to the edge of the channel where depths drop to more than 40 feet. Mullet, hardtails, squid, sometimes mackerel and small jacks school along the edges leading to the deep water. Divers can turn the corner and work their way up the jetties toward the tip in depths from five to 15 feet. Fishermen also work this area so divers need to take care not to conflict and, of course, prominently display a dive flag.

Jetty dives should be attempted only when clear water has been brought in by an incoming tide or at high tide. Only at high tide is the water both calm and clear. Spearfishing is not allowed.

Shore Dives

Aside from the jetties, the only shore dive of significance is the pilings of the old Crystal Beach Pier. These pilings can be seen from the beach road, roughly six miles east of Destin. The pier was destroyed by a storm several years ago, but the pilings remain and are home to tropicals, flounder, crabs, sand dollars, shells and an occasional octopus. The site is good for snorkeling since it is fairly shallow and usually offers little current. Diving at this location should be attempted only on calm days. There is a place to park at the pier area. Spearfishing is illegal.

Open Gulf

While the shipwrecks are Panama City's primary draw, the natural reefs are what have made Destin famous—even though there are plenty of artificial reefs and wrecks around.

The reefs lie in depths of about 60 feet and extend to several hundred feet.

These reefs of ancient coral limestone sometimes consist of low ledges only a few inches high to more than 20 feet. These ribbons of stone concentrate sea life. The reef systems include sponges, soft corals, anemones, small hard coral, sea fans, sea whips and other growth.

The ecosystems they form range from tiny baitfish to crustaceans, reef and pelagic game fish, rays, sharks, turtles and shells.

Due to depths daytime divers see these reefs in blue and gray.

Many divers go night diving on the reefs when underwater flashlights bring the reefs alive with their bright natural colors. The divers also get to see a number of nocturnal species rarely seen by day.

One could dive Destin reefs a lifetime and never explore them all. However, many are well explored and frequently visited. Following is a listing of the more popular reef systems.

Amberjack Reef

The Amberjack Reef chain consists of a series of ledges in 75 to 80 feet of water. They are about three and a half miles out, located at the base of a tall sand hill. They are popular for their abundant sea life. There are a number of locations in the area. 13711.3/47124.7

Triplett's Reef and Tyner's Spot

This system is made up of three reefs that are three and a half to four miles south southeast of the pass. They are in 72 to 75 feet of water. Reports are that the area holds good sea life. 13717.3/47125.0

Airplane Rock

It is two and a half miles out in about 75 feet of water.

Tri-Ledge

This reef consists of three parallel ledges. Each ledge is small, but the three are close together and stair stepped. All join at one end. They join at a spot called Dome Rock. This area is about 75 feet deep and four miles from port.

Timberholes

Twenty to 25 miles west southwest

SCUBATECH

DIVING CHARTERS & INSTRUCTION
• WRECK DIVING •
• REEF DIVING •

FOR THE NOVICE AND EXPERIENCED DIVER

RESERVATIONS: (904) 837-1933

(Charters leave daily, 7 days a week)

DESTIN STORE AND BOAT LOCATION

312 Highway 98
Captain Dave's Restaurant
on the Harbor
1/2 mile east of Destin Bridge
(904) 873-2822

THE SANDESTIN LOCATION

5371 Hwy. 98 • Sandestin
1/2 mile west of Sandestin Resort

HORSESHOE BEND
LIBRARY
DADEVILLE, AL

of Destin lies this huge reef area that gets its names from the holes pocked in the limestone reefs. Depths range from 100 to 110 feet. Timberholes holds tremendous fish populations, large lobsters, shells, turtles and other sea life. More or less directly south of Navarre Beach, this reef area has ledges that can reach to near 30 feet. A deep dive which limits bottom time, but worth an occasional trip for the multitude of sea life. 13480.8/47074.6

Nicky Grounds

Another large reef system south southwest of Destin, in the same general direction from the pass as the Timberholes. About 19 miles from the pass. Depths range around 100 feet. Perhaps not quite as dramatic as the Timberholes, but still a dramatic dive with lots of sea life. 13501.2/47074.7

Southwest Ridge

Another reef line to the southwest of Destin pass. At just over 20 miles, this area is somewhat further offshore than Nicky Grounds and Timberholes. 13541.0/47035.4

Rogers Hill Reef

These limestone ledges lie about eight miles southwest of the pass, with depths of 80 to 90 feet.

Matador Gully

This reef is just over 2.5 miles off Fort Walton Beach, and probably draws its name from the Matador Condominium. The gully reef is slightly more than six miles south southwest of the pass in less than 70 feet of water. 13640.0/47137.0

Big 16 Reef

This reef has a nice profile and lies in just under 90 feet of water. It is fairly near the wreckage of a liberty ship. It lies approximately seven miles southwest of the pass. 13647.2/47107.2

White Hill Reef

This limestone bottom lies about five and a half miles southwest of the pass, and has several spots of artificial reef rubble. Depths range around 75 to 80 feet. It also is in the same general area as the liberty ship. This area gets a lot of fishing pressure, so populations of large game fish come and go. Another spot near the liberty ship is known as Anchor Rock, in 85 feet of water. 13648.5/47116.6

The 18s

This long reef system is a combination of low hard bottom interspersed by several higher ledges. The reef area runs for miles east and west at 10 to 11 miles south of the pass and in 100 to 110 feet of water—much of it in roughly 18 fathoms. The area gets significant fishing pressure, but continues to hold good populations of game fish and other sea life such as moray eels, octopi, shells and lobster. 13677.5/47077.5

Southeast Rocks

These spots are slightly north of The 18s, and in slightly shallower water. They also are almost due south of Destin.

Long Reef and Big Reef

A series of staircase ledges, 200 yards long in 80 feet of water. Scattered tall ledges with lots of overhangs. Some snapper, shovel-nose lobster, lots of baitfish and shells. The area is three miles south of Destin and known for a few lobster and shells.

South Reef or Cabana Reef

This near shore reef lines in 75 to 80 feet of water and only two miles out the pass, almost due south. The reef is often visited by divers and, thus, gets picked clean. Still, it is an easily reached spot when time is at a premium or a north wind keeps the boats from going further out. On some days five and six boats of divers can be seen on this spot. Even so, there still are some groupers living in the crevices and flounder in the fractures. 13706.1/47130.1

Frangista Reef

Named for the Frangista Beach area, east of Destin, about seven and a half miles down the beach. Depth is about 80 feet. 13784.1/47121.4

Seagrove and Grayton Beach reefs

These reefs lie off the shoreline villages of the same names. They lie east of Destin 18 to 25 miles. The Seagrove reef lies in less than 60 feet of water, while the Grayton Beach reefs range in depth from 65 to 80 feet. The Grayton Beach reef offers ledges of 10 to 12 feet.13900.8/47085.7

Pyramids

These reefs lie about four miles off Phillips Inlet, with ledges dropping from about 55 to 75 feet. A lot of sea life.

These are just the better known and larger reef areas frequented by Destin divers. There are literally hundreds of other reef dives in water ranging from less than 60 feet to beyond the reach of sport divers.

A lifetime of diving would only scratch the surface.

Artificial Reefs

Fishermen and divers for years have used artificial reef material to enhance reef locations or to build a secret, private spot a little distance from a natural reef.

The idea was to put the reef near an area where sea life population would quickly build up, but that would not receive diving or fishing pressure from anyone except the builder. That way he could be assured of quality game fish whenever he chose to fish or dive there, provided he properly managed the harvesting and that no one accidentally stumbled over the spot.

In addition, there is plenty of military hardware on the gulf floor. Not unusual considering the amount of military training that takes place in the area.

A tulip shell perches in wreckage of the liberty ship off Fort Walton Beach

Photo courtesy of Captain J's Dive Shop, Destin, Fla.

Several of the dive shops favor the private artificial reef spots for spearfishing trips over natural reefs. The private spots, particularly, tend to hold more big fish because of the limited pressure they receive.

All the artificial spots quickly develop plant growth and heavy fish populations.

Following is a list of the better known sites.

Boxcars

The area has several sets of boxcars dumped to create fish havens. They can be found in a half dozen locations ranging from more than 15 miles to the southwest to about two miles and 75 feet due south of the pass. Sites include:

13554.8/47067.7	13555.0/47065.4
13665.0/47135.0	13715.1/47130.9
13773.1/47132.1	

Southwest

An area of junk lies about 18 miles south southwest of Destin. The wreckage includes remains of a boat wreck.

Red Missile

Lies in 115 feet of water about 12 miles southwest of the pass. Reports of good game fish inside the missile. 13625.0/47081.4

Airplanes

Wreckage of several planes lies scattered on the bottom around Destin. One is to the southwest about 14 miles, while another is in about 70 feet of water almost six miles off. Another is reported to be between the two. Another lies less than two miles southwest. A couple of planes lie in the vicinity of hard bottom off Grayton Beach. The area holds good fish populations and lobster.

Old Fishing Pier and Pole Spot

This artificial reef is about four and a half miles southwest of the pass in about 70 feet of water. This area holds a number of fish, and is a favorite area for fishermen to fish with live bait on unweighted lines for mackerel. 13662.8/47138.9

Bridge Rubble

Lying about two miles south and just east of East Pass, this spot is a favorite location for sport and certification check-out dives. It is about 60 feet deep and visibility usually is good. On summer weekends the area can get so crowded that boats have to jockey for position. However sea life accumulated quickly on the concrete rubble and a good population of sea life—shells, sand dollars, flounder, grunts and sport fish—hangs in there. The rubble was dumped in scattered mounds, making this a broad artificial area. 13718.8/47130.0

June's Dunes

This large artificial reef area lying southeast of Destin is a mile to mile and a half across. It includes car bodies, tires, a motorcycle and other debris. At 60 feet, the area holds grouper, amberjack, tropicals, baitfish, shells and flounder.

At least two books listing Loran numbers are available in Destin area stores. Their listings of artificial reefs seem to go on forever—washing machines, car bodies, military scrap, airplane wings, barrels, tires, grocery buggies, you name it.

Each artificial reef location draws shells, sand dollars, tropical and baitfish, reef fishes, pelagic fishes and, in some cases, significant lobster populations. Those with taller profiles often hold good amberjack and cobia populations.

Wrecks

While not known for its wreck diving as is Panama City, Destin doesn't take a back seat in that department. Following is a listing of Destin's better-known wrecks.

Whiteman Tug

This 100-foot tug was sunk in 1987 about 24 miles southwest of Destin. Due to its depth and distance it does not get heavy diving pressure. 13501.7/47030.4

West Liberty Ship

Off Navarre Beach, this 440-foot-long liberty ship holds amberjack, lots of grunts and other reef fishes. The ship is about 18 miles south southwest of the pass in 80 to 90 feet of water. 13505.4/47084.2

Butt Head Tug

This tugboat is sitting upright in 75 to 85 feet of water, approximately 12 miles southwest of Destin. It is considered an excellent fishing spot. 13570.2/47102.6

Ozark Target Ship

This one is listed just for the record, not as a prime dive opportunity. This large (315-foot) intact ship lies 28 miles southwest of Destin in 180 feet of water. Good for fishing. 13602.3/46967.1

Liberty Ship Thomas Hayward

This 440-foot-long, 57-foot-wide liberty ship is six and a half miles from the Destin pass in about 85 feet of water. Broken in the middle, the ship lies among a large area of hard bottom to both the north and south. The ship is a gathering place for shells, sand dollars and a variety of sea life. Tropicals and baitfish abound. The ship is well known to divers and fishermen and, thus, gets a good deal of pressure during the warm months. The ship holds game fish in numbers remarkable to the amount of pressure they get. However, at times of year the fishing pressure does take its toll, limiting the sea life population to smaller fish.13648.1/47115.8

Landing Craft

This military landing craft lies in 105 feet of water southeast of the pass approximately 16 miles. The craft is a dramatic dive, holding lots of baitfish as well as game fish. 13786.2/47054.9

Barges

A number of barges are used for checkout training dives, fishing and sport dives. Following is a listing of the better known barge dives.

Navarre Barge lies in 70 feet of water, about 17 miles west southwest of Destin. 13518.0/47111.9

Diamond Barge lies in almost 120 feet of water southwest of Destin pass. The barge is considered a good spearfishing dive, with large grouper reported inside the barge. 13544.2/47062.7

Butler or **Fort Walton Barge** is in 65 feet of water about four and a half miles west of the pass. The 200-foot barge is called Brown's New Air Force Barge is about five miles southwest of the pass, lying offshore of the Ramada Inn. The 100-foot barge rises about 18 feet off the bottom, which is at 70 feet. The barge was put down in the early 1990s and growth already is accumulating rapidly. Barge by some. There is some artificial reef material nearby. 13660.1/47134.1

Air Force or **Eglin Barge** lies in 60 feet of water about a mile and a half, south and just east of the pass. This 100-foot barge is near the bridge rubble and one of the boxcar artificial reefs. 13720.8/47132.6

The gulf floor is littered with wrecks and wreckage amid the reefs of Destin. Each has its own unique profile and sea life. All are prolific developers of ecosystems.

A boater traveling in any direction can hardly help but run over some of these spots if he only keeps a close eye on his depth finder.

Sometimes it is worth an unscheduled stop. The sea floor here holds a multitude of surprises.

A Queen Angel holds close to a limestone reef, encrusted in soft and hard corals and other growth. Such reefs are common from Destin to Pensacola.

Photo courtesy of Captain J's Dive Shop, Destin

Pensacola

The Area

This city on the bay would have beat out St. Augustine for the distinction of being the nation's oldest, continuously inhabited city had not the first settlement been abandoned after a few years.

This major seaport and population center of the Florida panhandle lies roughly 40 miles west of Fort Walton Beach on U.S. 98. An interesting excursion on the way is to take the tall bridge over Santa Rosa Sound at Navarre Beach and follow the beach road for 20 miles or so to the resort community of Pensacola Beach.

The road follows brilliant secluded dunes, past beach homes and condominiums and through a public beachside picnic area. At the Pensacola Beach end of the drive is a community of dining, lodging and recreation establishments.

Turn north here, go back over the sound to rejoin U.S. 98 for the trip into town. Actually the beach road continues eastward to Fort Pickens, but more on that later.

Even if Pensacola wasn't America's oldest city, it does date to the early 1500s and since has been under the flags of the Spanish, French, British, Confederacy and the good old U.S.A.

Each left its unique mark on the city, and some flavor from each can be found in the Preservation District where more than 500 homes of varying architectural styles have been faithfully restored.

Adjacent to the historical homes district is the downtown with its Seville and Palafox Historic Districts. There the visitor will find a collection of outstanding restaurants and unusual shops and boutiques. The nearby Historic Pensacola Village brings the city's colonial period to life with its attractive homes and museum complex.

As a full-fledged city, and one with a significant commercial shipping and industrial base, Pensacola lacks the compactness of Destin and Fort Walton Beach. Visitors will find four distinctive areas to the city:

1. Pensacola Beach is a resort community with similar entertainment and beach resort offerings as Panama City Beach and Destin/Fort Walton Beach, although it is a more compact and perhaps more modest in its number of offerings.

2. The community of Gulf Breeze sits on a neck of land bounded by Santa Rosa Sound to the south and Pensacola Bay to the north. It is home to dive shops, interesting shopping communities, restaurants and marinas.

3. Pensacola proper consists of the industrial and fishing docks along the bay, with the historical districts spreading northward from the waterfront. Further north the city becomes more industrial.

4. Naval base and Big Lagoon area. This area is west of Pensacola proper. First is the naval base to the immediate north and west of the Pensacola Bay pass (west of the downtown), followed by a series of marinas, docks and a great restaurant or two along the waterfront of Big Lagoon and the intracoastal waterway.

The shipping and naval base provides a distinctive seaport flavor to this town—a unique military air, great bars, sometimes rowdy entertainment all tied together with a patriotic flair.

Where to stay

Like other resort cities of the region, Pensacola offers everything from budget motels to luxury condos. Excellent beach front accommodations are available to the southeast of Pensacola at Pensacola Beach and to the southwest at Perdido Key.

A number of hotels are dotted around the bay, with convention and business style hotels located on the city's major thoroughfares.

In the summer season, beach front accommodations command the highest prices, with inland property prices about the same as in other southern cities.

Several hotels in the historic district put visitors within walking distance of a number of dining, historic and entertainment spots, although probably will require a brief automobile drive to a boat dock for a dive trip.

In addition, camping is available at Fort Pickens on Santa Rosa Island and at Big Lagoon State Recreational Area on the west side of town.

Pensacola dining

This northern gulf city has been a commercial fishing port for many years, with several commercial fish markets hugging the northern rim of the bay.

Seafood, again, is king.

Greek, Cajun and old fashioned southern style cooking can be found in abundance. The water—bay and gulf—seem to draw good restaurants. It makes them easy to find. Just follow the roads fronting the beach and bay and your choices will be plentiful.

There are a couple of spots that some would call mullet houses to the west of town that could be easy to overlook.

Rusty's near Big Lagoon and The Original Point at Innerarity Point are two "old Florida" eateries that are much more than mullet houses. In between is the Oyster Bar Restaurant overlooking the intracoastal waterway and it is much more than an oyster bar.

Of course Pensacola has all sorts of franchised and fast food restaurants.

What to do
when you aren't diving

Visiting sites of several pre-Civil War forts can take a visitor back through 400 years of history. At Fort Pickens and Fort Barrancas Civil War relics remain, and the North Hill Preservation District is the site of early British and Spanish forts.

The Naval Live Oaks archaeological site helps trace the history of the region's early inhabitants.

There is canoeing and tubing on Coldwater Creek, Blackwater River (state recreation area), Perdido River or the Sweetwater-Juniper.

Big Lagoon State Recreation Area is a great spot for camping, hiking and picnicking.

A trip to Pensacola wouldn't be complete without a trip to the Pensacola Naval Air Station, "Cradle of Naval Aviation." It is home of the world-famous Blue Angels and the National Museum of Naval

Aviation, one of the world's largest air and space museums and the most important collection of naval aviation aircraft and memorabilia in the world.

There is plenty of water for bay, pier, surf and deep sea fishing. In addition, other water activities—boardsailing, jet skiing, sailing—abound.

There are plenty of tennis, racquetball and championship golf courses in the area. Pensacola has a greyhound track offering paramutual wagering.

Colossus, one of the largest lowland gorillas in captivity, calls The Zoo home. Located just east of Pensacola, the zoo also offers 600 other animals on 30 acres.

For more information on Pensacola activities, accommodations and dining, contact **Pensacola Convention and Visitor Information Center, 1401 East Gregory St., Pensacola 32501. (904) 434-1234 or 1-800-343-4321.**

Pensacola Diving

The Pensacola diving community—among the most active along the northern gulf coast—has witnessed a great deal of change in the past 20 years.

The old flagship—Skipper's—has closed and been replaced by a number of new, well stocked, progressive shops scattered across the city.

Eight shops now call Pensacola home, some under common ownership. They range from waterfront shops with their own boats to modest, neighborhood shops serving mostly the local market.

Following is a list of the shops, their addresses and phone numbers:

**Dive Mart
5501 Duval St.
Pensacola, FL
(904)494-9800**

**Gulf Coast Pro Dive, Inc.
7203 Highway 98 West
Pensacola, FL 32506
(904)456-8845**

Gulf Breeze Pro Dive
207B Gulf Breeze Parkway
Gulf Breeze, FL 32561
(904)934-8845

Pensacola Scuba Inc. (PSI)
1813 B. Creighton Road
Pensacola, FL 32504
(904)478-1020

PSI Diving Co.
300 Pensacola Beach Boulevard
Gulf Breeze, FL 32561
(904)934-5009

Southwind Dive Shop
33 Gulf Breeze Parkway
Gulf Breeze, FL 32561
(904)932-2224

Scuba Shack
719 S. Palafox St.
Pensacola, FL 32501
(904)433-4319 or (904)433-3483

The Dive Shop
13111 Sorrento Road
Pensacola, FL 32507
(904)492-3483

Most of the shops offer frequent dive trips—just as fast as they can load the boats and make their runs to the wrecks and reefs during the season.

And, they will go on extremely short notice any other day of the year that weather permits.

Always check ahead to check on weather and reserve a spot. Boats fill up quick at certain times.

The captains in this area know reef areas and can offer an array of dive opportunities from wrecks, natural and artificial reefs. Some offer fishing opportunities as well as diving.

Two-tank dives typically range from $40 to $50, with three-tank dives ranging to about $65.

As with other ports along the northern gulf rim, Pensacola offers boat ramps and marinas for visitors who wish to dive from their own boats. Again, please remember that the gulf is no place for the novice fresh-water weekend boater.

No one has any business in the open gulf without loran, compass, depth finder, ship-to-shore radio, a good chart, up-to-date weather information and some idea of where he or she is going.

There are several marinas in Gulf Breeze and across town in the Big Lagoon area.

The sole outlet to the gulf is Pensacola Pass to the southwest of downtown. It is a broad, deep channel used by every type of craft from aircraft carriers to runabouts. If you are in the runabout, keep your eyes peeled. You will be the little guy and you will be the one who has to get out of the way.

Following is a listing and brief description of Pensacola's favorite dive spots.

Bay Dives

Pensacola Bay is a deep, sprawling bay spanned by several long bridges and with several arms spreading eastward from the mouth. Big Lagoon and the intracoastal waterway joins from the west.

Active with commercial shipping, Pensacola Bay generally is too murky for much diving, especially in its upper reaches.

However, there has in recent years been some extremely specialized archaeological diving in an effort to learn more about the fleet that went down more than two centuries ago in a hurricane. The wrecks are beneath several feet of silt, however.

Near the mouth of the bay are several good dives that can provide reasonable visibility on an incoming tide or at slack high tide.

Tugboat Sport

Wreckage of this tugboat can be reached by boat or from shore. It lies just past the entrance to Gulf Island National Seashore. Local dive shop operators or authorities at Fort Pickens can help locate the exact spot.

DIVE PENSACOLA

GULF COAST PRO DIVE	GULF BREEZE PRO DIVE
(904) 456 - 8845	(904) 934 - 8845
7203 HWY 98 W.	207B GULF BREEZE PKWY.
PENSACOLA, FL. 32506	GULF BREEZE, FL. 32561

PENSACOLA'S SCUBA PROFESSIONALS

DIVE THE BEAUTIFUL WATERS OFF OF AMERICA'S OLDEST CITY WITH OVER FOUR AND A HALF CENTURIES OF HISTORY. PENSACOLA'S WATERS ARE RICH WITH HUNDRED OF WRECKS INCLUDING THE NAVY'S SECOND BATTLESHIP THE USS MASSACHUSETTS

TWO FULL-SERVICE FACILITIES INCLUDING CHARTERS, SALES, RENTALS, CLASSES, AND GEAR REPAIRS.

OPEN 7 DAYS A WEEK, 363 DAYS A YEAR AND EAGER TO SERVE YOU!

SHERWOOD

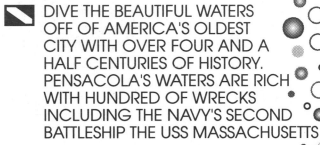

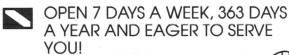

Fort Pickens Jetties

These jetties that protect the western side of Pensacola pass are a popular dive spot that can be reached from shore and by boat. The rocky bottom slopes to a depth of more than 50 feet and is covered with sea life. As with all passes, tides can be strong and this dive should be undertaken near high tide or at slack high tide. Access road to Fort Pickens leads westward from Pensacola Beach. There is only one road in and out, so you shouldn't get lost.

Shore Dives

Catherine

The broken wreckage of this old sailing ship lies in 15 to 20 feet of water near the west end of Santa Rosa Island, near the old Coast Guard station. The ship went down in a storm in the early 1900s. The wreckage is close to 300 yards off shore, so be prepared for a hearty swim. Actually this dive is much more easily reached by boat. The wreck does lie outside the surge line, and is badly deteriorated. Tropicals, flounder, spadefish and shells can be found.

Pensacola Beach Wreck

Wreckage remains of an old tug boat lay in 15 to 20 feet of water east of the Pensacola Beach water tower. Check local dive shops for the exact location and whether the wreckage is covered by sand. It holds tropicals, flounder and, sometimes, small snapper.

Pilings

A series of pilings laying on top of the sand are west of the fishing pier on Pensacola Beach. They reach into the gulf for 40 or 50 feet and sometimes attract flounder.

Open Gulf

Like the rest of the northern gulf, open gulf diving is what draws enthusiasts to the region.

And Pensacola sports enthusiasts—led by efforts of the Escambia County Marine Recreation Committee—have worked hard to make sure that there are plenty of varied diving opportunities in the area. They have developed dozens of wreck and artificial reef sites over the past few years, and continually add to those sites or develop new ones.

So near the deep DeSoto Canyon, Pensacola offshore waters usually offer exceptional visibility. With many of the wrecks located in waters of 100 feet or less, two-tank dives give divers plenty of bottom time.

This far west, near-shore natural reefs are beginning to thin out and most of the natural rock is in close to 100 feet of water and deeper. While many divers visit the natural rock, this diving center thrives on several dramatic wrecks and artificial reefs.

Wrecks

There are a mixture of wrecks placed on the bottom by those trying to enhance sea life habitat, and by mother nature claiming old, damaged and weak craft.

These craft are great attractors of massive schools of fish, shells, sand dollars, sometimes lobsters and other sea life.

U.S.S. Massachusetts
Lying two miles outside Pensacola pass, this pre-World War II dreadnought lies in 25 to 30 feet of water. It was sunk there in the 1920s. On June 10, 1992, the Massachusetts was named a state underwater archaeological preserve, with a bronze plaque affixed to the forward gun turret. There will not be marker buoys attached, but the ship is easily located since it is awash at low tide. To ensure decent visibility and to avoid strong currents, a battleship dive should be scheduled for an incoming tide near high tide or at slack high tide. The ship is home to snapper, grouper, amberjack and most other reef fish. There are also tropicals, but shells are scarce due partly to heavy harvesting. 13215.0/47108.9

San Pablo (Russian Freighter)
Not really a Russian Freighter, this 400-foot ship sank in the 1940s after being towed to the Pensacola area for repairs. It has been hit by a torpedo in the Florida straits during the war. She lies in 75 feet of water, about nine miles southeast of the pass. The ship holds an incredible amount of baitfish and grunts. There also are populations of grouper, barracuda, snapper and other reef fish. 13263.8/47077.1

Liberty Ship Joseph L. Meek
This is another of the series of liberty ships purposefully sunk off the northern gulf coast to help build sea life habitat. This 480-foot

ship lies seven miles east southeast of the pass in 80 feet of water. Put down more than 15 years ago, the ship holds the same type sea life as the freighter. Depth is 80 feet. 13306.9/47103.3

Sylvia

A 65-foot-long tugboat sitting in approximately 80 feet of water. Lots of shells and sand dollars are around. The wreck, eight miles south southeast of the pass, holds good fish populations. 13253.0/47075.5

Deliverance

This is another 65-foot-long tugboat in 80 feet of water and in the same neighborhood as the Sylvia, and holds similar sea life. It too is about eight miles out the pass. 13247.7/47074.7

Heron/Elsie M LCM

The steel tug boat Heron sits upside down inside an LCM landing craft 11 miles south southeast of the pass. It wasn't planned that way, according to local divers, it just happened that way when they were building the artificial reef habitat. Approximately 90 feet. Lots of fish. 13253.0/47060.6

Brass Wreck

The local name given to the wreck of an old sailing schooner

Barnacles, urchins and an arrow crab crowd for space on the hull of the dredge Avocet, south of Pensacola.
Photo courtesy of Gulf Breeze Pro Dive, Gulf Breeze, Fla.

that lies in 85 to 100 feet of water 15 miles east southeast of the pass. The more than 150-foot-long turn-of-the-century ship got its name from the large number of brass artifacts found around it. Beams, ribs, ballast rock and steering gear remain. Lots of sea life including most reef species. 13365.9/47085.1

M.D. Whiteman

Another 65-foot-long steel tug boat. This one lies 17 miles east southeast of the pass. This holds similar sea life to other shipwrecks of the area, and possibly larger fish because it is farther offshore than the other tugs. 13501.7/47030.4

Supply Boat

A 180-foot supply boat lies in about 90 feet of water about nine miles south and just east of the mouth of the pass. It is in a fairly large artificial reef area, which means that other dive opportunities are close by.

Tug Phillip

This tug boat, put down in December, 1990, also lies about nine miles south and just east of the mouth of the pass. It is relatively close to the Supply Boat site, and is in 95 feet of water. 13256.2/47059.4

Tug Born Again

Another tug boat in the same general vicinity as the Supply Boat and Phillip, slightly west of the previous two sites. The wreck has been enhanced as a sea life habitat by artificial reef material dumped in the area. It also is about nine miles off shore and in 95 feet of water. 13247.6/47060.8

Dredge Avocet

The dredge is almost 250-feet-long and almost 70 feet tall, creating a dramatic reef that holds significant sea life. This dredge also lies south and slightly east of the pass in about 115 feet of water. Since the dredge stands so high off the bottom, much of the dive can be above the bottom depth. 13248.4/47007.2

Tessie

This 40-foot hull is more artificial reef than a wreck. It lies in 75 feet of water about eight miles south and slightly east of the pass. Several car bodies are in the vicinity. 13250.3/47078.5

Barges

Pensacola's barge dive opportunities, like those of Panama City, have been improved dramatically by an aggressive program of reef building.

Some area barges have been around for years, while sportsmen continually hunt surplus to add to the already numerous spots.

Area barges include:

Three Coal Barges lie less than two miles off the beach in 50 feet of water east of the pass about four miles. These three 200-foot barges lie end to end. They have been there for some time and hold excellent fish populations and other sea life. 13270.5/47108.0

82 Barge or Tex Edwards Barge lies about seven miles southeast of the pass with water 70 feet at the top. Tropicals abound, along with a variety of other sea life. 13300.4/47101.9

P.C. Barge lies about eight miles south southeast of the pass. It is in the vicinity of several tugboats and other artificial reef material that creates a large fish habitat area. Depth is around 75 feet. 13253.6/47076.3

Soule Barge lies in 82 feet of water and has other artificial reef material in the vicinity. It is about eight miles south and slightly east of the pass. 13248.0/47074.6

Jim Penny Barge lies in 65 feet of water northwest of the Russian Freighter about three miles. It is deteriorated badly, but frequently holds strong fish population. 13216.1/47074.2

Artificial Reefs

The aggressive reef building program in these waters makes it impossible to come close to listing all the dive opportunities.

The following sites highlighted are the largest, most well-known and most popular with divers.

All of these reefs hold good fish populations, shells, sand dollars and other sea life.

Casino Rubble

This wreckage is from an old Pensacola Beach casino that was torn down in 1972. It lies perhaps 15 miles down the beach from the pass, but only three miles off the resort community of Pensacola Beach. The concrete rubble holds flounder, some snapper and other reef species. 13333.3/47115.2

Bridge Rubble

The rubble from a dismantled intracoastal waterway bridge lies in 80 feet of water, six and a half to seven miles southeast of the pass. The concrete and steel rubble covers an area the size of two football fields and has the same sea life as other area reefs and wrecks. It also has an abundant shell and sand dollar population.13277.5/47091.8

CSX Rubble - Al Johnson Construction

This large artificial reef site built in 1987 by the Escambia County Marine Recreation Committee contains several railroad bridge spans, broken barge pieces and other rubble. It sits in 90 feet of water about nine miles off shore.13255.1-.7/47065.6-.9

Scrap Steel Site

This large area of steel scrap sites in water ranging from 65 to 90 feet in depth. The dump sites begin about seven miles out and continue south to about nine miles. They were put down in 1988.

13247.0/47081.6   13254.3/47082.8
13247.6/47076.5   13247.5/47068.1
13248.0/47062.4

ARCOA Reef Modules

These two sites were built in 1989 in 80 to 85 feet of water seven or eight miles south and slightly east of the pass. The spots are only yards apart. 13251.5-2.0/47068.8

Monsanto Boxes

These four-foot-by-four-foot prefabricated plastic boxes were deployed in 1989 in 65 to 70 feet of water. About 200 of them lie fairly close together about seven or eight miles south of the pass.

13248.6/47081.2   13246.7/47079.7

Preform Concrete Units

These culverts are in 80 to 90 feet of water about nine miles south to slightly east of the pass. They were deployed in 1988 and 1989.

13248.7/47068.8   13254.7/47069.2

The Silos

These fiberglass tanks were deployed in two locations, one at 117 feet south and slightly east of the pass, and the other in the same direction in 124 feet of water. Both were deployed in the fall of 1990. 13248.9/47004.4

Gulf Power Towers

These large towers are at two sites, one in 77 feet of water and the other in 82 feet of water. The towers are in the same general area, south and slightly east of the pass. 13253.0-.2/47082.5-.6

Air Transport

A 128-foot long airplane rises almost 30 feet off the sand seven or eight miles east southeast of the pass. It is in about 75 feet of water about five miles off the beach.

A-7 Jet

This jet plane lies about 17 miles south of the pass in 110 feet of water.

Tenneco Oil Rig

This drilling tower was declared obsolete by an oil company and donated to the public as an artificial reef in 1982. It was sent to the bottom about 22 miles off shore. The tower is a maze of metal cross beams standing well off the bottom. The top of the rig is at 80 feet, while the bottom is in 175 feet of water. Thus, divers should confine themselves to the upper sections of the rig. 13324.7/47012.6

Airplane

An airplane wreck lies in 75 feet of water about three miles west of the Russian Freighter. Other wreckage can be found in the vicinity.

Natural Reefs

Big Rocks

Behind the liberty ship and about 10 miles east southeast of the pass is a large area of natural reefs known as the Big Rocks. This area consists of old coral heads and coral encrusted rock ledges. Depth ranges around 90 feet, and all sorts of sea life is abundant. The are lots of shells, reef fish and lobsters. This series of reefs is scattered over a large area and shows little pattern.

Green's Hole

This limestone reef in 110 feet of water is one of the Pensacola areas best known. The circular ledge is a fine place for lobsters, reef fish and shells. 13279.9/47061.6

Timberholes

This massive reef system is part of the same group of limestone ledges described in the Destin/Fort Walton Beach chapter. The system lies about half way between the Pensacola and Destin passes. The reef gets its name from the rocky area pocked with circular holes. There are a couple of popular theories regarding formation of the holes: one is that these holes were where trees once stood in prehistoric forests—when the ocean floor was once dry land; the other is that the holes are the effects of erosion on rocks that once were an ancient shoreline—rocks pounded for thousands of years by surf before waters rose and left that ancient shoreline 100 feet beneath the surface. Whatever the case, divers report that lobsters love to crawl in the holes for cover. The reef is in 105 to 115 feet of water. 13441.4/47068.2 (many others in area)

Paradise Hole

This reef lies about eight and a half miles southeast of the pass in 95 to 100 feet of water. 13292.7/47085.5

96 Hole

This large reef area consists of three- to four-foot ledges is in 90 feet of water. Common sea life includes flounder, snapper, grouper, angelfish, grunts, turtles, moray eels and some lobsters. 13303.8/47099.0

CM Reef

This large reef area has ledges similar to those of the 96 Hole, and is home for similar sea life. It is about 14 miles out and in depths between 90 and 100 feet.

Dutch Banks

This long series of low ledges begins just west of the Pensacola Pass and continues to within about six or seven miles of Perdido Pass. The ledges have caves and certain areas are covered by beautiful sea fans. At about 70 feet and so near shore the area gets a great deal of fishing and diving pressure, thus fish populations can be erratic. However from time to time good populations of snapper have been spotted. 13130.7/47079.1

Near Russian Freighter

This area of hard bottom and coral heads is about five miles from the Russian Freighter and within a mile of some artificial reefs. Depth is about 80 feet. 13288.3/47070.4

Other Reef Areas

Nowhere do the cliffs descending into the DeSoto Canyon come closer to shore than due south of Pensacola Pass. At less than 20 miles off shore the bottom drops away at a precipitous rate into depths of hundreds of feet.

Perhaps this geologic feature—the dominating canyon of the northern gulf—accounts for the large areas of ancient coral heads found once depths reach 95 to 100 feet and extending southward to the drop-offs.

These reefs hold great fish populations, shells, lobsters and other sea life. Due to their depths, bottom time is limited and divers often favor shallower dives.

However, for experienced divers who don't mind limited bottom time, these reefs are virgin diving territory offering dramatic scenery, lots of sea life, and great visibility, sometimes to 100 feet or more.

Gulf Shores/ Orange Beach

The Area

Less than an hour from Pensacola is Perdido Key and the Alabama state line. It is an interesting drive through pineywoods forests before climbing a high bridge over the intracoastal waterway at Innerarity Point.

From atop the bridge the gulf waters spread out to the south, while the white sands and pine forests of Perdido Key stretch east to Pensacola Pass and west to Perdido Pass. Beyond, further to the west, lie the Alabama resort communities of Orange Beach and Gulf Shores.

Much of the region owes its development success to a hurricane—Frederic, which blew away many of the old beach cottages that dotted the shoreline prior to the 1979 storm.

In their place rose shining new condominiums, restaurants, water parks, marinas and other beachside entertainment.

Perdido Key is split by Florida and Alabama. The narrow barrier island has seen dramatic condo growth in the past decade, with several fine restaurants also making the key their home.

This side of Perdido Pass has a distinctive family-vacation air, with several beachy shopping communities scattered along the key.

In addition, one of the region's most "famous" night spots (day spot too, for that matter)—the Flora-Bama Lounge. It is, of course, on the state line, with the club technically in Florida, with Alabama getting credit for the parking lot. The Flora-Bama looks to have been built in stages, which it was, and now has fine live entertainment. It also is home for the mullet throwing championship with one of the coast's most famous personalities, former University of Alabama and NFL quarterback Kenny Stabler often throwing out the first mullet.

Another tall bridge spans Perdido Pass, the channel that connects Perdido Bay with the Gulf of Mexico, and the major outlet for fishing and dive boats.

The beach road is spotted by restaurants, night entertainment, marinas, beach stores, shopping centers, condos, hotels, a sprawling state park and sparkling white dunes from the pass to the resort town of Gulf Shores where the development reaches its peak.

Two decades ago the community of Orange Beach was little more than a handful of fishing docks on a neck of land sticking out into Perdido Bay.

But how things have changed. This community encompasses not only that neck of land, but also the beach area to the east and west of Perdido Pass. Fishing and diving boats, upscale marinas, ship stores, restaurants, night life and beach shops make this one of the best kept beach secrets of the northern gulf.

The community merges with Gulf Shores to the west, which has been Alabama's beach playground for years. Almost a decade and a half after the hurricane, Gulf Shores is a mature resort with many shops, entertainment, recreation, lodging and dining facilities.

The Alabama coast continues another 20 miles or so westward before reaching the mouth of Mobile Bay, which marks the end of the crystal white beaches and a beach highway paralleling the coast.

Where to stay

Hotels and condos line the beach front, with only intermittent interruptions, from Perdido Key through Gulf Shores. In between are cottages, privately owned and chain motels.

Beach front properties in summer are the most expensive, with a few inshore motels charging somewhat less.

Gulf State Park has a beach front hotel, but also offers cottages around a lake and a huge campground.

The Alabama coast offers almost 8,000 units for rent, which

often sell out during the summer months, spring break and other holidays. So make reservations to assure the place you want.

Some condominiums offer up to four bedrooms for large groups, and virtually all condos offer full kitchens, as do many of the hotels.

Larger properties offer tennis, health clubs, swimming pools—some indoor—beach pavilions and rentals, plus golf at a place or two.

The 468-site state park campground is enhanced by several private camping facilities on the gulf and around the bay.

There are dozens of rental agencies in the area. For a copy of publications listing properties for rent contact:

—Alabama Gulf Coast Area Chamber of Commerce at (205)968-7511.

—Orange Beach Chamber of Commerce (205)981-8000.

—Perdido Key Area Chamber of Commerce (904)492-4660.

What's to eat

Yep, seafood again.

But not every great restaurant is on the beach, although many are. Every location along the coast has those special restaurants with their special recipes. The Alabama and extreme west Panhandle area of Perdido Key is no exception.

There is a distinctive Cajun flavor that has drifted over from the nearby Mississippi and Louisiana bayous. But good southern cooking still dominates.

There are enough Tex-Mex, fast food, fried chicken and buffet spots to satisfy every teenager in the world. They are everywhere these days.

There also are some spots you should look out for.

Don't forget The Original Point Restaurant at Innerarity Point where the floor is made of tiles that don't match but the food is perfection.

And Hazel's killer breakfasts are not to be missed.

There's fine dining at a second-story restaurant at Perdido Pass where the view of the pass opening to the gulf is as fine as the food.

While not a mainstream food place, the Pink Pony on the beach at Gulf Shores is a must-stop for a cold brew after an afternoon of beach time.

In between are lots of great places to eat—from Kirk Kirkland's Hitchin' Post where you can get great ribs and steaks when you can't look another fish in the eye, to Zeke's Landing Restaurant overlooking Cotton Bayou to the Original Seafood and Oyster House where you can see the restaurant's pet alligator.

The choices are plentiful along the beach, along the back bay road and north on Alabama 59 to Foley.

What to do
when you aren't diving

Hang out on the beach, for one thing. People watching is great and the water is inviting.

Once parched, there is fresh-water fishing, nature trail hiking, golf, tennis and pier fishing within Gulf State Park.

Another great nature hike can be found at Bon Secour National Wildlife Refuge west of Gulf Shores on the road to Fort Morgan. It is a great spot for bird watching in spring and fall.

This road takes the visitor to Fort Morgan, overlooking the eastern side of the mouth of Mobile Bay. It was a major part of the Civil War Battle of Mobile Bay and was surrendered to Union forces during that battle in 1864. This was the battle in which Admiral David Farragut issued his famous line, "Damn the torpedoes. Full speed ahead."

The fort is open for tours, along with a museum on the grounds.

Back in town, there are mini-golf courses, water parks, bike rentals and other roadside entertainment spots scattered about. A 16-acre zoo north of town offers 200 animals from alligators to zebras.

Sailing and fishing charters are available at several marinas, along with parasailing for those who think it's fun to be pulled into the air by a boat while wearing a parachute.

Diving the Alabama Coast

The waters off the Alabama coast are a continuation of the fine diving opportunities of Pensacola waters. With the Pensacola Pass and Perdido Pass only a few miles apart it is somewhat arbitrary to include some spots in one chapter and not the other.

Fact is, divers from both ports find themselves often diving the same reefs and wrecks.

This chapter deals only with those dive spots from half way between Perdido and Pensacola passes to the eastern approach to

Mobile Bay. There also are some excellent dives off the mouth of Mobile Bay to slightly to the west of the mouth of that bay.

They will be addressed in a separate chapter.

There are three dive shops in the Gulf Shores/Orange Beach/ Perdido Key area. All offer air, equipment sales, rental and repair and dive charters.

Following is a list of the shops, their addresses and phone numbers:

Pleasure Island Dive Center
474 East Beach Boulevard
Gulf Shores, AL 36542
(205)948-6883

Underwater Connection II Inc.
Highway 180 at Sportsman Marina
Orange Beach, AL 36561
(205)981-5585

Down Under Diving Shop
809 Gulf Shores Parkway
Gulf Shores, AL 36542
(205)948-DIVE

The shops maintain long hours and offer frequent dive trips during the summer months, but some may trim hours during winter. Call ahead. In summer, an advance call will help assure you a spot on a dive trip. In winter, shops can help make advance arrangements for a trip, since they are not as frequent in the cooler months.

Two-tank dives typically range from $40 to $50, with longer offshore trips ranging to $60 or more.

There are a number of marinas to service private boats around Perdido Bay, particularly north and east of the pass. The area offers several launch ramps capable of accommodating large pleasure boats.

As always, if you plan to dive from your own boat, know what you are doing. Have the appropriate safety and navigation equipment.

Perdido Bay's sand bars and winding channels require close attention. The channel through the pass is deep and safe, provided the careful boater stays within it. Once outside the pass, the gulf is essentially barrier free.

Following is a listing and brief description of dive spots off the Alabama coast, east of Mobile Bay.

Bay Dives

Perdido Bay on its good days can provide interesting snorkeling, particularly around piers and at Alabama Point. Most diving takes place within site of the highway bridge at Alabama Point. The water grows too murky for decent visibility farther up in the bay.

Sheepshead and spadefish are plentiful around the rocks used to shore up the sand bottom around Alabama Point. Visibility frequently ranges to 15 feet or more.

Like the pass at Destin, Perdido Pass runs swiftly on an incoming and outgoing tide. Water is clearest and diving is safest at slack high tide.

Highway Bridge

The new bridge over the pass can be a good dive, providing great care is taken in dealing with sometimes heavy boat traffic and strong currents. The area sometimes is thick with fish, including speckled trout, flounder, sheepshead, white trout and grunts. A number of tropicals also can be seen. The depth under the bridge reaches 30 feet in the channel. Always pull a dive flag.

Sea Wall

The sea wall that runs along the east side of the pass extends to a depth of about eight feet. It has sea life similar to the bridge. The current along the wall also can be swift.

Jetties

At the mouth of the pass are jetties built to keep the pass from filling with sand. They can be reached from shore. Visibility ranges to 20 feet, sometimes more, at high tide. Depth ranges from four or five feet to about 20 feet at the tip of the west jetty. Ranging toward the channel divers should take extreme caution because the bottom falls away rapidly, there is a lot of commercial boat traffic and the current can be extremely swift. The jetties are home to many tropicals, flounder, mullet, sheepshead, occasional grouper, gray snapper and triggerfish.

The east jetty offers similar visibility to the west jetty. Depth ranges to about 30 feet at the point. Many divers prefer this as a close-in boat dive, anchoring on the lee side of the weather and swimming up to the rocks. Some divers say it seems that shells are more plentiful on this jetty than the west jetty.

Shore Dives

Whiskey Wreck

This may be the northern Gulf of Mexico's best shore dive, especially since recent erosion has left more of the ship uncovered than any other time in recent history. Also called the Mail Wreck, this Norwegian lumber boat was blown ashore in the hurricane of 1906. It lies about 120 yards off shore. It was rumored to be a rum runner. It lies in 15 to 20 feet of water, parallel to the beach in broken sections over a 100-yard area. Portions of the hull, some metal and timbers remain. Flounder, sheepshead, tropicals, spadefish and butterfly fish in summer are common. Check local dive shops for exact location.

Piers

A much more recent hurricane, Frederic, which devastated Gulf Shores more than a decade ago, ripped away a number of fishing piers along the coast. Some were rebuilt. Some weren't. But everywhere the piers once stood are now piling stumps. Some stick above the water line; some are below. Shells, sheepshead, flounder and sand dollars can be found around the pilings. Standing piers that are popular with divers include those at the Pink Pony and Sea & Suds. There also is a pier at the Day's Inn Motel, which some divers say provides a good night dive.

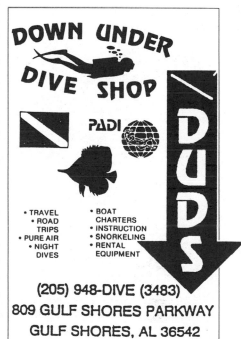

DOWN UNDER DIVE SHOP

PADI

DUDS

- TRAVEL
- ROAD TRIPS
- PURE AIR
- NIGHT DIVES
- BOAT CHARTERS
- INSTRUCTION
- SNORKELING
- RENTAL EQUIPMENT

(205) 948-DIVE (3483)
809 GULF SHORES PARKWAY
GULF SHORES, AL 36542

Open Gulf

Like Pensacola, most natural reef diving takes place fairly far off shore and in depths in excess of 100 feet. But thanks to an aggressive reef-building program there are countless artificial reef and wrecks to dive in much shallower water.

The artificial reefs develop sea growth rapidly, and hold dramatic sea life populations.

One phenomenon enjoyed by fishermen and divers alike is the incidence of the much-sought-after red snapper. A decade ago the species was so depleted that charter fishermen had to popularize several species once scorned to keep their customers happy.

Thanks to creel and size limits imposed several years ago, red snapper are again plentiful off the Alabama coast.

These prize fish seem to adapt extremely well to artificial reefs, perhaps even more than to large natural reef areas.

Wrecks

A number of shipwreck dives are available off the Alabama coast.

The Whiskey Wreck shows up as a long, dark smudge against the seaward side of the sand bar just off the Gulf Shores Beach.

Photo courtesy of Pleasure Island Dive Center

Liberty Ship Sparkman

Like other liberty ships sunk as fishing reefs in the northern gulf, the Sparkman holds a variety of sea life. It lies in 93 feet of water just over 17 miles southwest of Perdido Pass. 12948.1/47020.2

Liberty Ship Allen

This probably is the most frequently visited of the liberty ships by area divers. It is the closest and at a depth that provides adequate bottom time. It is in 80 to 90 feet of water and 8 miles south of the pass. 13069.2/47059.0

Liberty Ship Wallace

This ship is particularly popular with area fishermen and divers because it holds good sea life populations. It is in 90 feet of water and about 10 miles due south of the pass. 13038.0/47046.0

Lipscomb

This tug boat lies in 78 feet of water, 16.5 miles southwest of the pass. It holds amberjack, some grouper and typical reef fish. 12900.9/47045.0

Tulsa

This wreck is 32 miles southwest of Perdido Pass and almost due south of the mouth of Mobile Bay. It lies in 84 feet of water. 12711.9/47027.4

Liberty Ship Anderson

Another liberty ship, this one lying 31 miles to the southwest in 82 feet of water. It too is off the mouth of Mobile Bay. 12733.4/47018.6

Liberty Ship Edwards

This liberty ship also is about 31 miles southwest of Perdido Pass, and south of Mobile Bay. It is in 84 feet of water. 12709.4/47013.6

Dredge

The remains of a dredge lie just outside the mouth of Perdido Pass and in only 30 feet of water. It offers a variety of sea life and plenty of bottom time.

Tug Boats

There are two tug boats roughly 20 miles southwest of Perdido Pass. One is in 80 feet of water and north of the Sparkman, while the other is in 64 feet of water and somewhat inshore of the first. That tug is reported to be 105 feet in length. 12956.3/47021.7
12957.8/47039.9

Barges

As with other locations along the northern gulf, this area too has a number of barges that divers frequent for spear fishing, shell collecting and sight seeing.

The more popular ones include:

Upside Down Barge, covered with sea fans and sea whips, is about 10 miles south of the pass in 100 feet of water. It is partially covered by sand.

Three-Mile Barge lies fairly close, making for a short boat run. 13063.4/47087.1

Buffalo Barge lies in 54 feet of water 17 miles southwest of the pass. 12881.9/47045.5

Buffalo Barge Number Two is 18 miles southwest and in 66 feet of water. 12876.8/47044.3

North of Liberty Ship Sparkman lies a barge in 80 feet of water. 12979.5/47034.4

While they are not reality yet, a series of barges are being readied to construct an artificial reef several miles long from just west of Perdido Pass to a point offshore from Lake Shelby at Gulf State Park—a distance of about seven miles. The plan is to sink the barges in an east-west pattern, end to end, in 30 to 50 feet of water. The barges are to be sunk roughly two miles offshore as a sea life habitat within reach of divers and fishermen, particularly those operating in small boats with limited range.

Check with local dive shops to determine the status of this project. Once completed, these barges will almost immediately begin developing sea life and will provide divers with dramatic dive sites and lots of bottom time.

Artificial Reefs

There are literally thousands of artificial reef spots off the Alabama coast. One of America's most aggressive reef-building programs takes place in this area, and it has paid off in artificial habitat that offers some of the region's best salt-water angling.

Reefs popular with divers include:

Bridge Rubble

A new bridge was recently built over Perdido Pass. The old one was dismantled and dumped at several different locations in the gulf to form habitat. Dive shops report 13 different inshore spots that they visit, with others in deeper water. One, nicknamed Atlantis, provides a dramatic profile off the bottom and is a favorite of underwater photographers.

Lillian Bridge Rubble

These piles of bridge rubble went down years before the Perdido Pass rubble. They continue to hold good fish populations. In addition to the bridge rubble, the general area also is home to Kelley Pipes, another artificial reef. One area is nine miles south of the pass in 92 feet of water, while another is about the same distance out, but in only 60 feet of water. 13046.7/47062.8   13059.2/47054.9

Mobil Oil Platform

Lies due south of the pass in about 90 feet of water. This structure holds good reef fish and other sea life. 13070.0/47020.0

Gas Rigs

Off Mobile Bay spreading both east and west are gas drilling rigs. When drilling is taking place these rigs look like oil rigs, with a large superstructure standing high above the sea surface. Once drilling is complete, only a small structure stands above the surface. And there is much less structure beneath the surface than with the huge oil rigs off Mississippi and Louisiana. However these rigs still are worth a diver's attention. Divers report snapper and other species schooling in and out of the limited structure, and often in relatively shallow water.

Boxcars

Railroad boxcars have been dumped in several locations to create artificial reefs. These sites are about 10 miles off, south and slightly west of the pass. They lay in 90 to 100 feet of water.

Sea Lab Star Reef

This reef draws its name from the Dauphin Island Sea Lab, and lies in an area of artificial reefs southwest of Perdido Pass, more than 20 miles down the beach and perhaps 10 miles off shore. The area holds good sea life. Search for other locations. 12900.0/47019.4

Natural Reefs

Most significant natural reef areas are roughly 20 miles off shore. Depth on most spots in the vicinity of 100 feet or greater. The primary area, known as the Trysler Grounds, is a wide area of hard bottom, high ledges and ancient coral heads.

The area abounds with lobster, grouper, snapper, amberjack and other reef species. Shell collection also is good.

The area gets only light diving pressure because of its distance off shore.

There is a small amount of hard bottom near shore, which gets a good bit of diving pressure, but still makes for an extremely interesting dive.

Dutch Banks

This low ledge stretches east to west about seven miles off shore from just west of Pensacola Pass to just east of Perdido Pass. The reef is in about 70 feet of water and consists of low ledges, with some caves. The reef contains areas of beautiful sea whips and sea fans. 13131.0/47079.0 (many other spots in area)

Trysler Grounds

This large reef area lies roughly 20 miles due south of Perdido Pass, and is frequented by divers from both Pensacola and Perdido bays. Some areas are low rocky bottom attracting large populations of grunts, vermilion and white snappers, while other spots are high ledges holding nice populations of red snapper, grouper and amberjack. In fact, some of the Gulf of Mexico's largest amberjack, in excess of 100 pounds, come from these waters. Fishermen have enhanced the reef area with their own artificial reef spots, ideal for spear fishing when located. To be as far off shore as it is, this area gets significant fishing pressure from private boats. Not that it is recommended, but on a calm summer weekend a boater wouldn't need even a bottom finder to locate reefs. Just look for the boat clusters. Charter and private boats share these reef areas. But if you are in a private boat and private boats share these reef areas. But if you are in a private boat remember to observe common courtesies and not move in on a sport where someone already is fishing. 13100.0/46990.0 to 13060.0/47000.0

Southeast Banks

This hard bottom lies 28 miles southwest of Perdido Pass, and much nearer the mouth of Mobile Bay. This hard bottom holds significant sea life, but visibility is sometimes limited by murky water coming from the bay and some silt on the bottom. Depth is about 75 feet. 12808.3/47027.0

Cobia, also known as Ling swim with spadefish over the Three Mile Barge off Gulf Shores, Ala.

Photo courtesy of Pleasure Island Dive Center

FUN SCUBA LESSONS
"HIGH QUALITY WITHOUT THE HIGH PRICE"

"Professionals in Diver Education"
INSTRUCTION • SALES •
TRIP RENTALS • REPAIRS   PADI 5 STAR
Indoor Heated Pool

SPECIALIZING IN
INDIVIDUAL & SMALL
GROUP PACKAGES

928-5550
UNDERWATER WORKS INC
Located on Hwy. 98 Montrose
between Fairhope and Daphine

VISA   MasterCard   AMERICAN EXPRESS

057

Mobile/ Dauphin Island

One of the South's great historical port cities, Mobile lies at the northwest end of Mobile Bay and is a great jumping off point for diving the Gulf Shores/Orange Beach area, Dauphin Island or the Mississippi Coast.

It is about an hour northwest of Gulf Shores and is a major seaport for commercial shipping.

It also is a city of historical significance, with its French and Spanish influence tied more to New Orleans than the Alabama upstate cities of Montgomery, Birmingham and Huntsville.

Mobile Bay itself is too murky for diving. And while Dauphin Island is a neat port, it lacks dive facilities. There are several charter fishing boats on the island, and there are excellent launch facilities for private boats. A diver must have a boat to dive out of this side of the bay or make special advance arrangements for a charter.

But back to Mobile.

This city on the bay has three distinct parts for most visitors.

1. The eastern shore really isn't Mobile, but many Mobile workers call the eastern shore home. This eastern flank of Mobile Bay consists of a string of communities scattered over high ground overlooking the bay. These communities of Point Clear, Daphne and Fairhope offer fine restaurants, arts communities, bed and breakfasts, shopping, touring, and one of the South's truly great accommodations of the old style—the Grand Hotel at Point Clear.

2. Downtown Mobile offers a mild flavor of the New Orleans French Quarter with its wrought iron balconies and narrow streets. Its history goes back to the 1700s and the recreated Fort Conde serves as an excellent welcome center to the city. The downtown area also offers beautiful old southern homes and ancient oaks overhanging the roadway. The state docks are part of the downtown scene, with huge ships coming and going down the narrow channel.

3. West Mobile. There has been dramatic residential and commercial growth to the west of downtown. There are malls,

entertainment, dining and hotel districts along Airport Boulevard and I-65. Location of the interstate, the convenient dining and lodging make this an ideal area for divers wishing to stay in Mobile to take advantage of diving both Mississippi and Alabama coasts.

Accommodations in the area can range from the lavishness of the Grand Hotel to some motels along I-65 that go for $30 per night or less.

Dining opportunities, as with any big city, range from fast food drive throughs to chain restaurants to local establishments that have wonderful reputations for dishes they have developed.

Seafood, Cajun and Creole dishes are specialties of Mobile.

Area leisure activities include the usual golf, tennis, bayside fishing, sailing, museum and old home tours.

In addition, the Battleship Alabama—now a permanently docked historical tourist attraction—is one of the state's most popular attractions. The ships and dramatic loading facilities of the state docks make an interesting tour. Bellingrath Gardens, south of the city and on the way to Dauphin Island, is one of America's most beautiful homes and gardens. Plants are in bloom every month of the year at this 800-acre estate.

On the Alabama coast west of Mobile Bay, the fishing and shrimping villages of Coden and Bayou La Batre are worth a drive and stroll. There are a couple of great seafood restaurants in the area.

Dauphin Island is just off the Alabama mainland and is the western boundary of the mouth of Mobile Bay.

The Island offers a public beach, several motels, several restaurants, charter-boat docks, boat ramps, campground and Fort Gaines, which houses a modest museum of Civil War artifacts and a well-trained staff to tell you about the fort's history.

A ferry connecting Dauphin Island with Fort Morgan on the opposite side of Mobile Bay makes for an interesting excursion to the beaches of the eastern half of the Alabama coast without having to travel back through Mobile.

Diving off Mobile Bay

There are three dive shops in Mobile, the nearest locations for air, equipment, repairs and rentals. All are well-established shops, having been in their present locations for a number of years.

While diving out of Dauphin Island is not the easiest thing in the world, if there is a way to get a charter out of that port, these dive shops can do it for you.

In addition, there is one dive shop in Daphne on the Eastern Shore.

Following is a listing of the dive shops, their addresses and phone numbers:

Davey Jones' Locker
1857 Government St.
Mobile, AL 36606
(205)479-2550

Deep Sea Dive Center, Inc.
7131 Airport Blvd.
Mobile, AL 36608
(205)343-DIVE

Gulf Coast Divers
1284 Hutson Drive
Mobile, AL 36609
(205)342-2970

On the Eastern Shore:

Underwater Works Inc.
Highway 98
(P.O. Box 1320)
Daphne, AL 36526
(205)928-5550

The shops can arrange trips out of Perdido Bay, and other northern gulf locations. They work with established dive boat captains. Trip costs can range from $45 to $70, depending on the length of the trip and number of dives per trip.

Diving off Mobile Bay essentially involves boat diving. Several of the liberty ships, and the southeast banks listed in the Gulf Shores/Orange Beach section are more quickly reached out of Mobile Bay.

Other locations most quickly reached from Mobile Bay include:

Gas Rigs

These rigs can be seen standing offshore. Those engaged in drilling operations are large and look similar to the oil rigs off Mississippi and Louisiana. Others are but stubs jutting above the surface, where drilling operations are completed. These have much less structure than the drilling platforms, but reports are that even these smaller structures hold significant fish populations. The larger platforms hold good fish populations, including reef species, and, on some, trout, redfish and sheepshead.

Dauphin Island Bridge Rubble

Hurricane Frederic severely damaged the old Dauphin Island Bridge. A new bridge was built and the old one was carted into the gulf where it was dumped over a large area about 10 miles south and slightly west of the bay mouth. The rubble holds large fish populations, including the prized red snapper. The rubble piles are sufficiently scattered that divers could visit the area a number of times and never dive the same spot twice. The rubble is mainly concrete and in 60 to 80 feet of water.

12697.9-8.8/47051.7-.8	12708.7-.9/47050.5-.6
12691.2-.9/47049.7-50.0	12703.6-5.7/47046.6-7.2
12711.8-3.7/47039.4-42.2	12724.9-8.4/47039.0-40.9
12719.9-23.8/47037.7-8.5	12715.2-8.6/47035.7-7.1
12723.4-4.9/47035.1-6.6	12726.7-35.3/47035.0-6.9
12719.2-20.5/47034.5-5.5	12709.7-.9/47038.7-.8
12717.0-.5/47040.2-.5	

Drydock

This artificial reef of old drydocks holds large fish and is popular with both fishermen and divers. It lies south of Mobile Bay in just over 70 feet of water.12704.6/47028.7

Butterfly fish mix with grunts and snapper around an artificial reef. The scene is reflective of wrecks and artificial reefs off the northern gulf coast from the Florida panhandle through Mississippi.

Photo courtesy of Gulf Coast Pro Dive, Pensacola

Mississippi Coast

The Area

Long ignored by divers frequenting the nearby Alabama and northwest Florida ports and the Louisiana oil rigs, Mississippi is beginning to be recognized as a destination for oil rig diving.

And, there are a number of other wreck and artificial reef sites that hold excellent fish and shell populations.

As the oil rig opportunities become better known, Mississippi should grow as a diving destination. That is because the best rig diving involves longer trips offshore to reach the clearer water no matter whether diving off Louisiana or Mississippi. Sea life is excellent on the rigs, on either side of the state line.

Historically, Mississippi's drawback as a sport diving destination is that the artificial reefs and wrecks are much further from port than along northwest Florida and Alabama. The reason is that clear water usually is found only outside the barrier islands lying 10 miles off the Mississippi coast. Between the islands and the mainland is a shallow, soft-bottom sound that is generally murky.

Also complicating visibility even further offshore are the outflow of the Mississippi River to the west, Mobile Bay to the east and a number of smaller rivers in between. When those rivers are putting out lots of fresh water the gulf is murkier. Seas and winds also can influence where that murky water goes, causing visibility to vary more than other locations.

The trip westward from Mobile to the Mississippi coast is intermittently lined with pineywoods and marsh. It takes but a few minutes to Pascagoula—famous for its ship building and a Ray Stevens' tune about a squirrel in church—and adjoining community of Gautier (pronounced Go-shay).

Leave I-10 and drop south onto U.S. 90, which hugs close to the shoreline for virtually the entire length of the Mississippi coast, finally turning slightly inland toward New Orleans. Beyond Gautier, it quickly cuts through the beach communities of Ocean Springs, Biloxi, Gulfport, Long Beach, Pass Christian, Bay St. Louis and Waveland.

For years the Mississippi tourism industry has labored hard to provide the best possible coastal resort communities possible. There always has been a smattering of fine restaurants, quaint shops, souvenir stores, marinas and motels to service beachgoers.

The generally murky sound waters, held in by the string of barrier islands off shore, and beaches with heavier mud content—requiring occasional shipments of sand to be brought in—kept these beaches from developing to the extent that those in neighboring Alabama and northwest Florida.

But in the past year something has happened to change all that. This beachside stretch of resorts is booming. The whole area looks far more prosperous than ever before. Fine restaurants, new hotels and motels, interesting shops and seaside attractions are blossoming everywhere.

Mississippi legalized dockside casinos, and Las Vegas-style gambling arrived. The law is worded so that these casinos are aboard permanently docked ships or boats. There are reports that customers line up and wait their turn just to get inside on weekends when numbers exceed fire code limits.

As the numbers of visitors increased, diving, fishing and other water sports and tourism activities have reaped benefits as well.

What's there to do?

The Mississippi coast has always had a rich offering of activities. The beautiful antebellum home of Confederate President Jefferson

Davis is open for tours. The home, two museums and veterans cemetery on the beach front are open daily.

There is horseback riding at A-1 Horse Riding Stables in Biloxi. Also in Biloxi is day sailing on a schooner, a 70-minute shrimping trip and boat excursions to the barrier islands.

In Gulfport is a 35-foot fishing boat that takes visitors on 10-minute trips to fishing spots, an amusement park, water parks and a dramatic Marine Life Oceanarium where trained dolphins and sea lions perform. It also includes a giant reef tank and a touch pool.

Because the Mississippi coast is so compact, attractions along the entire length are reachable in a short amount of time.

Other popular attractions and their locations include:

—Fort Massachusetts on Ship Island, one of the last masonry coastal fortifications built in the U.S. and occupied by the confederates during the Civil War.

—Fort Maurepas, a replica of the original which was built in 1699 by the French as their first fortification in colonial Louisiana.

—Gulf Islands National Seashore/Davis Bayou at Ocean Springs offers exhibits, trails, camping, a historic fort, marsh tours, islands and beaches.

—Historical Walking Tour of Biloxi includes 20 historical buildings.

—J.L. Scott Marine Education Center and Aquarium features a 42,000 gallon main tank and 40 large aquariums with local marine life. Live and static displays and continuous video show in auditorium. Biloxi.

—John C. Stennis Space Center is the location for space shuttle main engine testing before used to launch shuttle spacecraft. Self-guided tour includes museum, facilities. Bay St. Louis.

—Bay cruises and excursions to the barrier islands are available from marinas at most of the major ports. Rates vary.

—Old Spanish Fort and Museum, built in 1718, said to be the oldest structure in the Mississippi Valley. Pascagoula.

—Scranton Floating Museum is a retired 70-foot shrimp boat turned into an environmental learning center with aquariums, nature displays and hands-on exhibits. Pascagoula.

—Seafood Industry Museum has exhibits depicting the growth and development of the Gulf Coast seafood industry. Biloxi.

The new dockside casinos are the area's biggest draw, and are destined to become more and more popular as visitors discover the many sport and recreation opportunities close by.

Accommodations

Most of the area's hotels, bed and breakfasts and condominiums are right along the shore, usually across U.S. 90 from the water.

Lodging ranges from mom and pop motels to upscale condos. Prices are similar to those of other beach resorts.

With the coming of casinos, there may be changes in vacancy rates and price structures. Since the casino phenomenon still is relatively new, it may be good to call ahead for pricing information and reservations.

Most of the major chains have hotels in the beach areas.

Dining

The fast food and chains are there.

And so are a lot of neat local places—some with great names and interesting fixtures, like the crushed ice in the urinal at Mary Mahoney's Old French House in Biloxi.

A couple of other interesting names include the Blow Fly Inn, The Rebel Dip, Toucan's Mostly Mexican Cafe, and Widow Watson's Restaurant.

Seafood, again, stakes its claim as king. But this area has a healthy sprinkling of steak houses, Italian, Chinese and Mexican eateries.

Ask the locals for suggestions. While tourists historically have not favored this area's beaches as they have of northwest Florida and Alabama, the region's fine dining never has had to take a back seat to any other area.

For more information on the Mississippi coast, call or write:
Mississippi Gulf Coast Convention & Visitors Bureau
Box 6128
Gulfport, MS 39506-6128
1-800-237-9493
(601)896-6699

Mississippi Coast Diving

There are four dive shops serving the Mississippi coast. Each offers air, equipment sales, but only some of them offer charters in Mississippi waters.

Following is a list of the dive shops, their addresses and phone numbers:

Dive Five
Edgewater Village, Suite 25
Biloxi, MS 39531
(601)385-7664

SeaSpace Dive Center
2707 Highway 90
Gautier, MS 39553
(601)497-1381

Sports Unlimited
173 Hardy Court Shopping Center
Gulfport, MS 39507
(601)863-5839

The Wet Set Pool & Dive Store
2112 Old Mobile Highway
Pascagoula, MS 39567
(601)769-8156

With dive trips further off shore along the Mississippi coast it is advisable to call a few weeks ahead to determine opportunities for a dive trip on a given date.

With most diving areas 25 miles or so out, longer runs and somewhat higher costs should be expected. A day of diving runs in the $75 range, and provides a significant amount of time on the water.

Boat ramps are available at several locations along the coast, but only the experienced salt-water boater should consider diving from his own boat.

The Mississippi coast offers a couple of challenges even greater than some other northern gulf areas:

1. Longer runs to reef areas, which means keeping a close eye on the weather since it will take longer to get back to port.

2. The 10 to 12 mile run to the barrier islands must be done carefully. The sound has shallows, which means that boaters must take care to stick to established channels.

Following is a listing of Mississippi coast dive spots.

Wrecks

Bill Walker

This wreck lies in 55 feet of water about six and a half miles from the entrance to Horn Island Pass. It was put down as an artificial sea life habitat in 1989. About 45 minutes from Pascagoula. 12441.3/47044.1

Marguerite

This wreck lies in almost 60 feet of water, between six and seven miles off Horn Island. It holds a variety of reef fish and shells. 12438.3/47043.2

WaterSpout

A wood-hull shrimp boat that sank in the mid-1980s after colliding with an oil rig. Pieces of hull and booms remain. 12428.9/47044.7

Shallow Liberty Ships

Two liberty ships were put down off Horn Island as sea life habitat in shallow water. Known as the shallow liberty ships, they are about three miles from Dog Keys Pass F.W. Buoy, and in about 45 feet of water. They are known as the Caldwell, at 12319.5/47061.5, and the Waterhouse, at 12320.1/47061.5. These ships create large artificial reefs that hold an abundant variety of sea life. Visibility can be weak at times. Snapper, triggerfish, spadefish and sheepshead are common.

Deep Liberty Ships

This 20-acre site contains three liberty ships that wree sink in 1978, plus a barge that was sunk in 1987. Two of the ships are broken in half. The ships are about 13.5 miles south of Horn Island in about 60 feet of water. With two of the ships broken apart, there are six loran coordinates, one of which is for the barge. The area holds significant fish population, including grouper.

12356.1/47030.8	12355.9/47030.8
12355.7/47030.5	12355.8/47030.3
12355.2/47030.4	12356.0/47030.8 barge

Joe Pennington Tug

This tug has been down for more than a decade, and holds sea life very well. Unfortunately the area off Horn Island sometimes has poor visibility. The tug is in about 100 feet of water.

Barges

These favorite artificial reefs of the northern gulf are present off the Mississippi coast as elsewhere off the northern gulf coast. Snapper, grouper and flounder are common. Visibility ranges from 10 to 50 feet.

Rubble Barge lies in 65 feet of water about seven and a half miles off Horn Island. 12403.7/47038.0

Bus Barge is a 90-foot-long barge lies in 60 feet of water seven or eight miles off Horn Island. The barge stands almost 20 feet off the bottom. 12404.7/47038.8

Hopper or Boxcar Barge stands about 12 feet off the bottom in about 70 feet of water. It is about eight and a half miles from the Horn Island Pass buoy. Several railroad boxcars and other artificial reef material are in the same area to create a larger artificial reef site. 12405.6/47035.5

Movable Barge sits in 65 feet of water almost eight miles from the Horn Island buoy. It stands about 12 feet off the bottom. 12405.8/47037.2

Dumpster Barge was sunk in 65 to 70 feet of water in the mid-1980s as a fish habitat. It is seven and a half miles out the Horn Island Pass. It stands more than 12 feet off the bottom. 12407.7/47038.3.

Ship Island Barge is a 195-foot-long hopper barge in 30 feet of water, about 5 miles from the Ship Island Pass #12 Buoy. It stands about 12 feet off the bottom at its highest point. 12227.4/47061.3

Swash Channel Barge also is 195-feet-long, and in about 40 feet of water. Lying on a mud and silt bottom, this barge rises about 12 feet off the bottom at its highest point. 12263.8/47063.2

Blue Wing, an ocean-going barge, lies in 65 feet of water 11 miles from the Horn Island Pass F.W. Buoy. The wreck holds a variety of reef fish, including red and mangrove snapper. Visibility can range from 10 to 50 feet. The wreck is an hour out of Pascagoula and an hour and a half from Biloxi/Ocean Springs. 12577.5/47035.0

Artificial Reefs

Boxcars and Rubble

A number of boxcars and other artificial reef material have been dumped in the vicinity of Hopper Barge, slightly more than eight miles from the Horn Island Pass. The rubble has been dumped in several locations around the barge to make a fairly large reef area with multiple locations. Depth is 60 to 70 feet.

12403.5/47036.8   12406.9/47036.3
12407.9/47035.5   12406.2/47035.5

Tires

An artificial reef made of auto tires lies in the same general rubble field as the Boxcars and Rubble.

Rigs to Reef Site

An artificial reef site designed as a dump site for oil companies to dispose of obsolete oil rigs. So far, no oil rigs have been dumped, but the site does contain a sea-going barge, deck barge and tug boat. The 650-acre site is 36miles south of Petit Bois Island in about 130 feet of water. The tallest wreckage stands almost 24 feet off the bottom. The area appears to be holding a lot of fish, and there is hope that coral will develop since there is some natural coral nearby.

12529.9/46920.6   12532.8/46922.5
12537.4/46922.7

Cement Modules

A series of about 100 cement modules create an artificial reef off Petit Bois Island, due south of the pass. Snapper and triggerfish are commonly seen in this square-mile site. It is just over 11 miles from the Horn Island Pass F.W. Buoy. Visibility ranges from 10 to 50 feet. 12404.9/47037.9

Ballast Rock Pile

This rock pile is only seven miles from the mouth of the Pascagoula River, and inshore of Petit Bois Island, making it one of the area's nearest dive sites. Flounder and stone crabs are common. The stones are about 10 feet deep, with visibility of about 10 feet. 12482.9/47077.2

Natural Reefs

Southwest Banks

This area of natural rock lies offshore near the Mississippi-Alabama state line. The area holds a good population of reef species. Depth ranges around 65 to 70 feet. 12650.0/47028.7

Oil and Gas Rigs

A number of these rigs lie off the Mississippi coast. While gas rigs begin showing up in the shallow gulf off Alabama, it is off Mississippi that divers begin to encounter the more dramatic oil rigs.

There also are the smaller gas rigs off Mississippi, and they are worth a dive, but they do not equal the oil rigs in size. And size of structure translates into amount and diversity of sea life that a rig will hold. On the positive side, a number of gas rigs are close to shore, about 18 miles out and only 6 miles off the barrier islands.

And even these smaller rigs have been reported to hold dramatic populations of large red snapper, plus amberjack, spadefish, an occasional grouper, triggerfish and, on the bottom, flounder.

Species that move in and out include sheepshead, speckled trout, mackerel, cobia, bluefish and redfish.

While the smaller rigs can be explored more quickly than the larger oil rigs, they still provide plenty of adventure, particularly for spear fishing.

Since a number of them are relatively close, divers can do a single-tank dive on one rig then hop to another for the second dive. While gas rigs look essentially the same from the surface, often each

OVER 20 YEARS EXPERIENCE

"Dive Into A New Dimension"

SEASPACE

NAUI SCUBA INSTRUCTION
Basic thru Dive Master
• Scuba Classes Held at YMCA
• Full Services Repairs & Rental
• Dive Trips & Travel
• Complete Line of Scuba Equipment
  Scubapro - Sherwood - Oceanic

RENT TO OWN AVAILABLE

VISA MasterCard

Dive Center

(601) 497-1381
2707 Hwy. 90, Gautier, MS

develops its own unique ecosystem—just as one reef may hold large populations of certain sea life, while another reef will hold a very different set of sea life.

Dive shops can run trips to the gas rigs, and captains lose no time getting to them since the location of each is well known. Boaters visiting the area should obtain location of the rig areas from dive shops or marinas before venturing out. Once in the area, a boater can find the rigs by sight. Check with local dive shops on whether it is allowable to tie directly to a rig or whether you must anchor off the rig and swim to it.

The larger oil rigs lie further off shore, requiring long runs—perhaps three hours—to these huge towers. Some of the more popular areas lie in 200 to 300 feet of water, which means divers must orient themselves to the metal rig, rather than to the bottom.

For practical purposes, this is diving without a bottom.

Rigs generally are found in patches. Thus, divers may choose to move from one rig to another for different dives during a single trip. However these structures are so large and hold so much sea life that many divers choose to spend their whole 4-tank trips at one site.

Oil rig diving holds a different set of safety criteria from all other types of diving in the northern gulf. For complete details on safety suggestions, diving tactics and special equipment, turn to the chapter on rig diving which begins on page 112.

Rig dives have a reputation for wonderful water clarity and huge populations of extremely large game fish. In addition to all the species that can be found in reef areas throughout the northern gulf, divers have reported seeing dolphin, wahoo, sailfish, blue and white marlin, tuna, whale sharks and other offshore species. Most of these are pelagic fishes and thus not found at every rig on every time. But because the rigs lie fairly far off shore and because of the depths, these fish do wander in and out of rig areas—probably because these rigs serve as underwater cafeterias.

Mississippi oil rigs, as those through Louisiana, have a haze phenomenon that has caused anxiety in more than one visiting diver. There often is a murky layer of water at the surface around the rigs. It probably is due to dirty water from the Mississippi River. Since salt water is heavier than fresh water, the dirty fresh water stays at the top of the water column, while pristine salt water lies underneath.

This murk layer can be anywhere from five to 15 feet thick. However, many a novice who has pulled up to a rig only to see this murk layer has suffered great disappointment before going over the side and finding the clear water underneath.

At some rigs there is another murk layer at the bottom (many rigs sit on soft bottom), but since the bottom is out of reach of sport divers it is an academic point.

A popular destination for Mississippi divers are the Horseshoe rigs in roughly 240 feet of water, and about three hours from port. While these rigs are sometimes surrounded by the surface murk, there is virtually always great visibility—100-feet plus—just beneath the surface.

These rigs are encrusted with soft corals, plants and crustaceans. In addition to abundant sea life, lobsters also call the rig home.

There are other oil rigs closer to shore in depths of 100 feet or less. While the boat trip to the rigs is less rigorous, divers must pick their days. The Mississippi River is by far the largest, but by no means the only river pumping cloudy fresh water into the gulf along this part of the coast. Thus, rainy weather hundreds of miles inland, winter runoff, wind blowing from certain directions, strength of tides and currents form a complicated formula that can make visibility around the close rigs brilliant one day and impossible the next.

Novice boaters should resist the temptation to attempt a rig trip without first doing it a few times with someone who has done it before. An oil rig is a big structure, and it is an occupied working platform. Supply boats can be coming and going, workers must be considered. Tying off requires a set of skills, and, for the diver in the water, there are a set of special considerations.

Once learned, these special skills are easily mastered by the proficient boater. But the uninitiated boater can get in trouble around an oil rig quicker than any other place in the gulf.

Divers wishing to book a rig trip through a Mississippi dive shop should check as far ahead as possible—perhaps a month ahead. These long trips cost somewhat more than the quick two-tank trips available off the Alabama and northwest Florida coast, but these are usually all-day trips and four-tank dives so the dives actually are a good value for what you get.

The key is to prepare for a long day on the water. Anyone prone to seasickness needs to take medical precautions. Everyone should dress appropriately and bring sufficient sunscreen. Plus, check with the shop or boat captain to determine who is bringing lunch. If a day on the water doesn't make you seasick, it will make you hungry.

Also, check with local dive shops on any special requirements they have of divers before allowing them on a rig trip, for any special equipment they require or strongly suggest, special protective underwater dress and any restrictions on what they will allow you to bring along.

Rig diving should be considered slightly more rigorous than reef and wreck diving, but not so much so that the average sport diver should be worried about it. The key is paying attention to and diving within the special rules required of rig diving.

The adventure is worth it. The volume and size of sea life is dramatic. These Mississippi rigs have been largely overlooked except by local divers and, because of the lack of pressure, make wonderful dives.

And, with the development of the Mississippi coast—thanks in large part to the casinos—this area is destined to quickly become a new center for oil and gas rig diving, with artificial reefs and wrecks to also be popular dives when visibility allows.

Petit Bois Island Gas Wells

These gas wells lie in 45 feet of water, about four miles from the Horn Island Pass F.W. Buoy. A variety of reef fish are seen. Visibility can range from 10 to 50 feet. 12509.2/47082.3

Horse Shoe Rigs

This patch of rigs lies roughly 60 miles south of Horn Island Pass in 240 to 300 feet of water, providing visibility of 50 to 100 feet. The rigs hold an abundance of tropicals, pelagic fishes, large grouper and other reef fish. It is a three-hour run from Pascagoula.

Getty Rigs

These rigs are 20 to 30 miles south of Horn Island Pass in 60 to 240 feet of water. They hold a diversity of sea life, including tropicals, pelagics and lots of reef species. Visibility can range from 20 to 100 feet. If the visibility is right, these rigs are a much shorter boat ride than the Horse Shoe rigs.

Louisiana Coast

Welcome to an area that, from the diver's perspective, is unlike any other.

Louisiana diving is oil rig diving, pure and simple.

Nowhere in the northern Gulf of Mexico can divers find spots where they can see as much sea life and as many record-sizes of sea life as that swarming around the oil rigs off the tip of Louisiana.

Asked if there were diving spots other than oil rigs off the Louisiana coast, one New Orleans dive shop operator paused a long moment and volunteered that there probably were lots of wrecks around. But with the oil rigs, he added, no one he knew had ever bothered to look.

But first things first:

The Area

From east to west, the Mississippi coastline drops away from U.S. 90 and the low swampland takes over. The highways—90 and I-10—cut past the shallow, broad saltwater lakes of Borgne and Pontchartrain and center on the Crescent City of New Orleans.

This major resort city is a hundred miles from gulf ports where dive boats depart for oil rig dive trips, yet it is the staging area for virtually all of those trips.

Some may consider that an inconvenience, but rarely do you hear complaints from divers who tie oil rig dive trips to shore time in

New Orleans.

The situation is this: While the dive boats are at the port communities of Grand Isle, Venice, Cocodrie and Fourchon, the nearest dive shops—equipment, repairs, rentals and air—are in the New Orleans area.

Thus, virtually every Louisiana oil rig dive trip begins in New Orleans.

Entire travel books have been written about New Orleans, so that effort will not be repeated here. As most everyone knows already, New Orleans is one of America's oldest cities, heavy in French and Spanish influence, famous for world-class dining, night life, the history of the French Quarter and Garden District of fine homes, trendy shopping in the entertainment district along the river and, most recently, a great aquarium that includes a huge saltwater tank with an oil rig habitat inside.

New Orleans' reputation for adult-style entertainment is well earned. It takes minimal effort to find great music, classic watering holes—some brewing their own beer, shows where entertainment involves people who wear very little, and places where happy Cajun music and dancing have crowds on their feet all night long.

Most also know that New Orleans is not just an adult vacation spot. The zoo, aquarium, riverboat cruises, swamp tours, museums, street music and Preservation Hall and historic battlefield are but a few of the sites that make this place a top family vacation destination as well.

Briefly, for those who have somehow missed this wonderful city, here is a quick overview from a guide published by the Louisiana Tourism folks:

The new business heart of the city is Poydras Street, a wide avenue stretching from the Mississippi River to the towering, silvery Superdome. Its glittering bustle is vaguely reminiscent of Dallas or Houston, Paris or London.

A short walk away is the Vieux Carre', the French Quarter, a place of narrow streets, wonderful old buildings, historical fascination and international beauty.

The French Quarter is the perfect introduction to the sights and sounds of New Orleans. There are many restaurants (famous establishments as well as modest cafes) numerous bars (large and small, noisy and quiet), and, of course, plenty of jazz at places like Preservation Hall and Maison Bourbon.

The Quarter is also a perfect place for long, slow walks, to peer through iron gateways into courtyards filled with lush tropical plants, ferns, butterfly lilies and banana trees, or to see an earlier time preserved in the Louisiana State Museum, the Historic New Orleans Collection, the Old Pharmacy Museum and others, as well as the many antebellum house museums. Endless shops offer everything from expensive art and antiques to fascinating junk. Or take one of the streetcars you'll find by the riverside to zip you upriver or down, for more browsing in the old French Market, or in ultra-modern Canal Place, Jackson Brewery and the Riverwalk. Also, don't miss the remarkable new Aquarium of the Americas, or boating to the Audubon Zoo.

Take time to explore the Garden District, a charming, historic neighborhood in uptown New Orleans. The streets here are wide, and the 19th-century houses have an openness, a public elegance that contrasts sharply with the narrow streets and closed courtyards of the Quarter.

Also in the Garden District is the beginning of a unique shopping district: Magazine Street. In converted cottages, dozens of small shops cluster randomly along the upper reaches of this busy street, selling a bit of everything: books and food, flowers and clothes, prints, art supplies and framing, and numerous antique shops.

The New Orleans area includes the neighboring cities of Slidell, to the northeast, Kenner and Metairie to the west and Marrero and Gretna to the south.

A hundred miles to the south lie the port outlets to the open gulf. Take U.S. 90 to highway 1. Go south of 1 to reach Port Fourchon and Grand Isle, the most popular departure point for rig diving. Take 90 to Houma before turning south to reach Cocodrie. And, take highway 23 out of New Orleans to reach Venice.

The route south through swamps, bayous, tidal streams and lakes is an adventure through one of Americas truly unique environments and cultures.

The ports are at the end of the roads. Except for Grand Isle these are exceedingly modest as tourist locations.

Grand Isle, on the other hand, is a significant gulfside resort, with a number of hotels and restaurants. It also has a reputation as one of the top 10 fishing spots in the world.

The seven-mile-long island offers sandy beaches, crabbing, boating, swimming, surfing, water-skiing and excellent bird watching.

Two lighted fishing piers are accessible to the handicapped. On adjacent Grand Terre Island are Louisiana Wildlife & Fisheries Marine Lab and ruins of historic Fort Livingston, which has no admission charge.

Grand Isle State Park is on the east end of the island. It is a 140-acre park with access to the gulf. It is a popular spot for outdoor activities and includes a 400-foot pier that is popular with fishermen.

Where to stay

First you have to make a decision—best done in consultation with the dive shop you are booking your dive trip through—whether to stay in New Orleans or at the coast.

If New Orleans is the choice, choices seem limitless. The French Quarter offers small, personal, historic hotels, towering modern hotels, condominiums, quaint bed and breakfasts. The Garden District also offers fine bed and breakfast opportunities. Many independent and most chains offer motels along the interstates and main city thoroughfares.

French Quarter area locations can be somewhat pricey, and visitors should check ahead to determine whether major sports events, conventions or other activities are underway. Rates tend to rise and accommodations can get tight around the time of significant events.

Accommodations outside the city center tend to be along the lines of those in other major southern cities.

Hotels and motels at the coast are similar in price to those of other coastal resort towns.

Some of the dive shops have special arrangements with hotels and motels, and some even offer special prices that include their own beach-house accommodations for dive groups. You may be able to save some money by checking with dive shops for dive packages that include accommodations.

Where to eat

This is world-class eating territory.

New Orleans is a melting pot of cultures, but perhaps the most famous is its Cajun cooking.

The city abounds with great dining opportunities—from expensive dining experiences unparalleled anywhere to unique neighborhood eateries with their own family-developed recipes.

If you don't get a great meal in New Orleans, it is your own fault. Tour books and tourist magazines list many of the areas fine restaurants. In addition, check with the locals. Tell them what you are looking for, the price range you want to be in and you will get plenty of choices.

While most places can be visited in casual dress, New Orleans does have places where a coat and tie are required. It is best to check in advance. Further, some places accept reservations, and others are strictly first-come, first-served. And many places have crowds almost every night so plan to make reservations, come early or wait in a long line.

Also, some of the areas best neighborhood restaurants are in neighborhoods that some would consider funky. If that's what you are after, check ahead about available taxis or nearby parking. Some places might make the uninitiated a little queasy after dark.

Bottom line, if you can't find it in New Orleans, it probably does not exist.

To the south, toward the coast, are many excellent Cajun restaurants, fish houses and other beachside-style restaurants, particularly in Grand Isle. Check with the locals for the best ones.

For more information on tourism, lodging and dining in this region there are several associations that can help:

Louisiana Office of Tourism
P.O. Box 94291
Baton Rouge, LA 70801-9291
(504)342-8119 or 1-800-33GUMBO

(State Tourism Centers are well staffed, well stocked and conveniently located. Stop by and they will load you up for free with information books, maps and discount coupons. Following is a list and general locations.):
—I-55 Southbound near Kentwood
—I-10 Westbound near Slidell
—I-59 Southbound near Pearl River

In addition, you can write or stop by the following locations for more information:
New Orleans City and Louisiana State Tourist Center
529 St. Ann St.
Jackson Square
New Orleans, LA
(504)566-5031 or (504)568-5661

Grand Isle Tourist Commission
Louisiana 1 at Santiny Street
Grand Isle, LA
(504)787-3700

Louisiana Diving

Seven dive shops in the New Orleans area offer oil rig diving. Some have common ownership.

These shops are well developed, offering air, equipment, sales, rental, repair and dive charters. Most have arrangements with dive boats on the coast, while one or two offers diving from their own boats.

Following is a list of the dive shops, their addresses and phone numbers:

Aqua Tech Dive Center
6101 Westbank Expressway
Marrero, LA 70072
(504)341-3483 or 1-800-878-6111

Harry's Dive Shop
4709 Airline Highway
Metairie, LA
(504)888-4882

Inner-Space High-Tech Divers
2929 Jefferson Highway
Jefferson, LA 70121
(504)833-8869

Outdoor Sporting & Scuba
6601 Veterans Blvd.
Metairie, LA 70003
(504)887-3483

Scuba Quest Sport Diving Center Inc.
3017 N. Causeway Blvd.
Metairie, LA 70002
(504)834-8243

The Scuba Company
7212 Hayne Blvd.
New Orleans, LA
(504)244-6292

The Scuba Company
1532 W. Lindberg
Slidell, LA 70458
(504)646-1919

Some of the shops offer oil rig diving year around, while others may offer trips only during the spring, summer and fall. Trips to the rigs are frequent during the warmer months, but due to the logistics—a long drive to the docks and a long boat ride from the docks to the deeper rigs—more advance planning is required than just walking aboard an open boat. Some shops say a week's notice is sufficient in summer, while others ask for two to three weeks. In other seasons, when trips are not so frequent, a month's notice is safest.

The shops deal with seasoned captains who know not only the gulf, but also the fine points of maneuvering around the oil rigs.

Since virtually all rig dives involve a full-day on the water, these are usually three- to six-tank dives. Prices range from $65 to $100 for a day on the rigs, with most shops commonly charging in the $80 to $90 range.

Several shops offer multi-day excursions that include food, ice, lodging, boat, air, tanks—everything—for a fee that runs $100 to $125 per person per day. Inquire about the package deals.

Boaters experienced with the gulf and with oil rigs dive from their own boats. However, casual boaters who are not experienced in this part of the gulf or with oil rig diving are strongly discouraged from diving from their own boats.

It is not that the rigs are hard to find. To the contrary, these vertical reefs stand high above the sea surface and are easily located by sight. There are a number of maps with rig locations that can be purchased, and once a boater gets into a rig patch area it is just a matter of picking out one to dive on.

The problems come in other areas:

1. Rigs have workers on them and there can be a lot of boat traffic. Iinexperienced boaters can get in the way or even in harm's way by improperly maneuvering around the rig traffic. Oil company workers are considered hospitable and normally don't order fisher-

men or divers away from rigs unless there is an important reason for them to get away. The experienced boater is quick to comply if asked to pull off a rig, since normally there is a good reason.

2. There frequently are significant surface currents around rigs. Those currents can shove a boat into a rig or create other problems for novice boaters trying to hook onto a rig.

3. Sea action. Some days the gulf is calm around the rigs, but other days it can be choppy and the combination of choppy water and its unusual action around a rig can make for tricky maneuvering, especially when trying to hook to the rig.

4. Boaters have developed several pieces of gear that they routinely use to ensure safe operations around the massive rigs. Some of that equipment a casual boater will not have.

In addition, there are the usual cautions of salt water, open sea navigation that requires special skills and equipment.

Oil Rig Diving

While other dive location chapters in this book have listed specific dive locations, this chapter is dedicated to only one kind of diving—oil rigs.

Thus, the chapter is devoted to the uniqueness of this type diving rather than discussing the subtle differences that divers find from rig to rig.

The rigs themselves are located in patches, in what some describe as east-west layers extending outward into the gulf.

Local rig divers have their favorites, where they consider sea life most abundant and visibility greatest. Some named West Delta 99A, 117G, 151 and 152.

Others highlighted the Mississippi Canyon Rigs—structures sitting in 400 to 1,000 feet of water on the edge of a significant northern gulf underwater canyon.

The numbers mean little to the visiting diver. To them two things are important: 1. That visibility is good and 2. That sea life is as abundant and large as advertised.

Of course, generally speaking, the longer the run off shore, the greater the abundance and size of sea life, and the greater the visibility. The closer to shore one dives, the closer he is to the cloudy water flowing out of the Mississippi River. Plus, the closer rigs get lots of fishing and diving pressure from private boaters.

Occasionally, trips are made to the near rigs. These trips may be an hour or slightly less from dock to rig. But more typically, oil rig trips take an hour and a half to three hours from dock to rig to assure the clearest water and best underwater scenery. While some, as those at the edge of the Mississippi Canyon, can sit in more than 300 feet of water, the most popular rigs are in 150- to 250-feet of water. Those are the ones far enough off shore to be in extremely clear water, yet close enough that most of the day isn't taken up by the boat ride.

Trips begin in New Orleans. Those are the shops booking rig trips and the nearest available air fills.

Most shop operators say they want to check C-cards, log books and to talk with the divers before a trip. They want to review safety rules, expectations and to talk through rig diving *before* the dive.

They want to know that the diver understands principles of buoyancy, current navigation, spearfishing, clearing a mask, hovering, plus having knowledge of equipment capabilities.

This diving is somewhat more rigorous than most other casual gulf diving, and the operators want to make sure both they and their customer is comfortable with what lies ahead.

The operators say they encourage divers to get some open-water experience—particularly open gulf experience—before tackling an oil rig. One, in fact, has developed a PADI approved rig diving course. It involves an evening of on-shore instruction, an instructor-accompanied rig dive, plus other experience dives. Other shops say they prefer, if not require, divers to have taken the underwater hunter course before turning them lose inside a rig with spear guns.

FISHING ◨ DIVING

Flipper II SINCE 1986

Provided: All Tackle, Fuel, Ice, Bait & Deckhands
- Local Fishing & Diving Trips
- 65' & 31' Fishing & Diving Boats
- U.S.C.G. Certified

888-4882
4709 Airline Hwy.

For Groups Up To 60

Once all is squared away with the dive shop, "hard core" divers spend the night in New Orleans, arise at 3 or 4 a.m. for the hour-and-a-half- to two-hour drive to the dock. Often, however, divers arrange lodging near the docks, drive down the night before and get a good night's sleep before the dive.

Getting Ready

This adventure is more than a quick excursion into the gulf. Rig dive trips take up the better part of a day, and some to the deeper rigs begin at dawn and last until dusk. Advance preparations are important for the length of the trip, and for special equipment that rig diving calls for.

In some cases, the dive shop or boat captain will provide food and drinks, but this normally has to be arranged ahead of time for an additional fee. Otherwise, bring plenty of food and drinks. A day on the water will make you hungry and thirsty. Pack something other than beer in the cooler. No dive master is going to allow a diver overboard if that diver has been drinking alcoholic beverages. Some boats do allow alcoholic beverages to be consumed on the way back to the dock after a dive—check this point ahead of time.

Oil rigs are rough, crusty structures. Local divers wear a Coon-Ass wetsuit—cloth gloves, long pants and long-sleeve shirt. This get-up will prevent abrasions.

Spear fishermen will want to customize their spear guns. Nylon lines are replaced with stainless steel. Otherwise, a speared fish will quickly cut off a nylon line by dragging it across a barnacle-encrusted beam and the spear will be lost.

Because of the size of fish that divers have the opportunity to spear, some choose to use a "riding rig." This term refers to a spear gun customized in the following way. The line normally connecting the gun and the spear is detached from the gun. The line still attached to the spear is replaced by stainless steel. To the end of the stainless steel line is attached a length of rope. On the end of the rope is a hook that the diver can attach to himself.

When the diver shoots a large fish, he hooks the spear gun over his shoulder and holds on to the rope with his hands while he rides down the fish. It offers two advantages—1. The diver has more maneuverability by holding onto a rope to fight the fish and 2. If the fish wins the battle and overpowers the diver, the diver can let go of the rope and has lost only the spear and cable, while saving the gun the rope and has lost only the spear and cable, while saving the gun itself which, hopefully, still is safely slung over his shoulder.

Offshore necessities should be gathered in advance: Sunscreen, a change of clothes, a hat, band-aids, aspirin and antiseptic cream, and maybe an extra spear gun spear if spear fishing is your main objective. Spear fishermen also prefer a stringer that they can hook to the rig, rather than having to take every individual catch to the boat. Bring a light if you want to gather lobsters. They like to hide in the rig's dark recesses. Some divers bring along a slicker to ward off the occasional shower—something important if you will be traveling in an open boat.

The Trip

Trips to the rigs can range from under an hour to three hours, with trips typically taking more than an hour. Dive shops use a variety of boats—from 100 feet in length to less than 30. Smaller boats typically are faster, noisier and lacking in amenities, while larger boats often are slower, smoother, quieter and offering more amenities.

Each type is right for a certain kind of trip. Decide what you are looking for and inquire of the dive shop the boat you will be going on before completing the deal.

A person can get seasick on a big boat as easily as a small one, so if you are prone to seasickness take precautions the day before your trip. The popular patch-behind-the-ear is an effective preventive, but requires a doctor's prescription. This means that you should check with your doctor before your trip about the advisability of using this medication, and obtaining the prescription. In addition, there are

LOUISIANA RIG DIVING TRIPS

INNER-SPACE HIGH-TECH DIVERS
* PADI Instruction - Entry Level thru Instructor
* IAND NITROX - Training and Support
* HIGH-TECH - Equipment Sales
* RIG DIVING - Training and Trips
* DAN O2 - Training
Visit our newly expanded SERVICE department
(504) 833-8869
Formerly VINEYARDS DIVE SHOP - owner Richard Haines
2929 Jefferson Hwy. Jefferson, La. 70121
UNDERWATER VIDEO AND SPEARFISHING ON THE RIGS

several over-the-counter seasickness pills available. Drug stores and dive shops usually carry one kind or another. Some cause drowsiness. Check side effects.

Whatever you choose, don't wait until you feel bad to take medication. It is too late then. Most medications must be taken some time before leaving the dock. Check the instructions.

The Gulf of Mexico is considered a calm sea, but rare is the day that it is perfectly calm. And the tip of Louisiana is well known for quick-changing weather, so what begins as a sunny calm day can end as a bumpy rainy day. Thus, do not expect a superhighway ride to the rigs.

The Rig

Miles before you arrive you will see your destination. The huge erector-set appearance of an oil rig platform—covering more than an acre of surface work area—looms high above the sea. Some rise higher from the sea floor than the Empire State Building, but standing alone against the vastness of the sea they can seem almost insignificant—from a distance.

There are close to 3,800 of these structures in the gulf. Off the Louisiana coast they are located in clusters, with the nearest ones visible from shore and the more distant ones 100 miles off.

Festooned with superstructure, the rig is a working platform. Work boats come and go. Permanent crews man the tasks required to draw crude deep from beneath the gulf floor.

For what rises above the surface of the sea, a great deal more lies beneath. Jackets—the name given to the massive stilt-legs anchoring the rig to the bottom—cross members, pipelines, cables, valves and steel structures create an angular jungle of hard structure for sea life to build upon.

The beams are holding places for barnacles, plants, soft and hard corals, shells, anemones and urchins. Nooks and crannies are home to lobsters and fish.

The entire rig beneath the surface is covered with life.

This plant and animal coating is the bottom of the life chain. Drawn to it are the larger species—barracuda, spadefish, snappers, groupers, sheepshead, mackerel, Spanish hogfish, a rare triple tail, tarpon, amberjack, jack crevalle, redfish, triggerfish, sharks, dolphin, cobia, octopus and a multitude of tropicals. The deeper rigs are visited by open sea species of marlin, tunas, dolphin, mackerels and such.

Visitors regularly comment on the abundance and size of fish found around the rigs.

A phenomenon that divers must get used to is that rig diving takes place within the confines of the rig itself, not in the outside fringes; and orientation is to the rig beams, not to the bottom.

The rig for biological purposes is not a single artificial reef, but rather a series of artificial reefs that change from depth to depth. Species change from depth to depth and area to area, with larger fish often (but not always) found at greater depths than smaller fish.

The Dive

As the captain approaches a rig a series of hurdles must be negotiated before the dive begins.

Surface currents are common and often remarkably strong. The captain must consider both wind and currents, approach the rig from a direction that wind and seas pull the boat away from the rig rather than push it into the rig.

Once within reach of the rig, it must be hooked and then attached by a bow line.

When the boat is safely secured, divers go over the side but still must fight the surface current to the rig itself and then find a handhold.

The dive takes place inside the rig, amid the maze of steel beams. At times divers experience a murky layer at the surface. At times there is no murk. Sometimes it is only four or five feet thick. Other times it can be heavy and extend to 30 feet beneath the surface.

DIVE! DIVE! DIVE!

into the unique and exciting underwater world of
Louisiana Rig Diving
Great vis!   Warm water!   Unusual Marine Life!

We offer personal service for small groups (6 persons) aboard our fast, comfortable, and fully equipped 26' boat. We provide soft drinks on the boat and offer an optional bed & breakfast package.

For more information call: **800-259-8443**
T.G.I.F. CHARTERS, INC. Grand Isle, LA

Beneath the murk the saltier water takes over and breathtaking visibility follows. Divers report being able to see completely across the rig's expanse.

As divers descend the surface current seems to lessen. They begin to scatter, based on activities. Tropical hunters spot their quarry and hover around the beams where these small aquarium species scurry in and out of protective cover.

Photography buffs seek out the pristine water and angles that frame their subjects. Favorite shots include close-ups of barnacles, corals, lobsters and encrusted beams, fellow divers swimming amid sea life and unusual or unusually large sea creatures.

The spear fishermen hunt for targets, sometimes venturing deeper than most others in search of the largest fish that they can find. While sightseeing, photography and tropicals collecting are growing in popularity, the majority of rig dives still are devoted to spear fishing.

Each diver chooses his own zone. While some spear fishermen move to deeper water and trade dive time for the chance as a record-size fish, others opt to stay shallower, conserve air and get maximum time under water. There is no correct dive. Rather, every depth is a different dive and the desires of each diver determines how far or how deep he roams.

When air is exhausted, care must be taken in returning to the boat. Carefully watch for other boat traffic. When returning to the dive boat, the diver takes a direct route to the ladder or grab line. A miss can make for a mess. Surface current can quickly carry a diver away from the boat, in fact some distance away before all the other divers can be recovered, the bow line detached and the boat turned to pick up the errant diver. It probably isn't particularly dangerous, unless the sea is significantly rough, but it can be disconcerting to a diver who watches his boat growing smaller and smaller as he is swept farther and farther away.

So don't goof off when returning to the boat. Know where you have to go. Go directly there. Get out.

Depending on the length of the trip, rig excursions once in a while consist of two-tank dives, but more commonly are three- or four-tank dives. On occasion, trips offer six-tank dives. Carefully documented surface intervals separate the dives.

Oil rig diving is not for everyone. There is the possibility that the size of the rig or the lack of bottom orientation could make some divers uneasy.

The length of the boat ride might make those prone to seasickness want to pass it up.

But to pass up this dive is to pass up the clearest water north of the Caribbean, and one of the few dives anywhere that a diver can pass through a series of ocean environments simply by dropping from one depth to the next.

And, only on the oil rigs can divers find such large examples of so many different species of sea life. And with such a wide variety of species—from tropicals to reef fish to pelagics to open sea marlins and tunas—all within a common framework.

Triggerfish and sheepshead maneuver in and out of the encrusted columns of of a Louisiana oil rig
Photo courtesy of Captain J's Dive Shop, Destin, Fla.

A diver descends into Vortex Spring, one of northwest Florida's best developed and popular for both training and sport dives. At Ponce de Leon, Fla., Vortex is but a brief diving distance from two other fine, commercially developed springs, Cypress and Morrison.

Photo courtesy of Gulf Coast Divers, Mobile, Ala.

Springs

The Gulf of Mexico is not the only place known for its fine diving along the northern gulf rim. Underground aquifers pour forth crystal clear fresh water in several dramatic springs.

Some are developed for divers; others remain primitive for the more adventurous diver seeking a new experience.

The sandy soil of the region soaks up millions of gallons of water and strains it into massive underground pools.

The water erodes the underlying limestone, carving tunnels to the surface.

In the springs are limestone cliffs and caverns for the more experienced divers.

The spring temperatures are cooler than the gulf in warm months and sometimes warmer than the gulf in cooler months. Temperatures usually range into the 70s, but can be slightly cooler. Flow from the springs can vary, depending on the amount of rainfall and the amount of water stored in the underground aquifers.

While water flowing from the springs is clear, heavy rain runoff temporarily clouds some of the pools. Thus it is best to check ahead before making a long trip.

The series of springs and the clear streams flowing from them range from fairly shallow to very deep. Some are compact, others sprawling. All are picturesque, with plant and animal life.

Some of the better-known fresh water dive sites in northwest

Florida include:

Becton Spring

This spring near the town of Vernon is about 35 feet deep and 100 feet across. The spring water gushes out from between huge boulders.

There are a lot of fish and plants in the spring area and along a fairly shallow but clear stream flowing from the spring.

According to local sources, from time to time there have been efforts to open the spring commercially. Presently, however, it is accessible only by water from Cypress Spring. See the Cypress Spring section for directions.

There may be other efforts to open Becton commercially again. Check ahead.

Blue Hole

In Florida Cavern State Park, this large spring area offers a bath house, camping and picnicking. The springs are along a run to the nearby Chipola River. Scuba diving is allowed. The state park is three miles north of Marianna on Florida 167. Best route out of Panama City is U.S. 231 North until you reach signs directing you to the park.

Cypress Spring

Cypress Spring actually is a series of springs boiling out into a pool that is more than 150 feet across. Depths range to about 25 feet and the stream flowing from the spring to Holmes Creek a quarter mile away is extremely shallow for the most part, and a popular canoe trail. The spring area itself has a lot of plant and animal life and is considered extremely picturesque, with visibility ranging to 300 feet.

The spring cavern offers depths to 70 feet. Entering the cavern through an oval shaped vent approximately 10 feet by six feet divers experience a remarkably strong flow. The cavern immediately opens up into a room approximately 40 feet wide and 14 feet tall.

The spring produces upwards of 90 million gallons of water per day into a pool where divers can see a number of freshwater fish, including freshwater mullet.

Owners of the spring and surrounding area have worked hard during the past several years to improve the spring and offer a number of amenities for divers, swimmers, canoeists and campers. Improvements scheduled for spring, 1993, are designed to make camping a comfortable outing.

The spring is three miles north of Vernon, Fla. Take Highway 70 two miles north of town and turn right down a sand road where a sign marks the way. From the north, the spring entrance is seven miles south of Bonifay.

There is a fee for diving and rental of equipment.

Marianna, Fla., Area Springs

There are several springs attractive to divers in the Marianna area. Two of the main ones are **Twin Sinks** and **Gadsden Spring**.

Gadsden Spring is deceptively small and dark looking from the surface.

It is only 25 yards across and water near the top is not so clear as water deeper down because of the lack of flow.

Once in the spring, a diver will discover a limestone cliff dropping 50 feet to a cave entrance.

Take Florida 275 four miles southwest of Marianna and turn left onto Florida 16. Go approximately two miles and turn left on a dirt road across from a gas station. Take a right on the first dirt road you come to—which should be about a half mile. Bear left when you come to a fork in the road. The spring is about a half mile from the fork.

Twin Sinks is a long pool with a spring at one end and a drain at the other. Depths range from five to 45 feet. Clarity is excellent.

Go southwest out of Marianna on Florida 276. Turn left onto Florida 167 and travel about four and a half miles where you should turn left onto a dirt road. Go approximately one mile and another short dirt drive leads to the pool.

DIVE *Cypress Springs* & *Canoe*

The Panhandle's Newest Dive Site!
A cool, clear spring pool hidden in the Florida woodlands.

Diving • Snorkeling • Swimming • Canoeing
Tubing • Camping

P. O. BOX 726, Vernon, FL 32462 **(904) 535-2960**

123

Merritt's Mill Pond

The dive actually can be considered as the whole five-mile run from the spring pool to the dam at U.S. 90. Below U.S. 90 the stream dumps into the Chipola River.

The Blue Spring, as the head is known, is a commercial swimming and diving center May through September with an admission charge.

There are picnic tables and a bathhouse. Scuba diving is not allowed in the spring pool itself, although snorkeling is. Scuba can be used through the rest of the five-mile run to the dam.

Fresh water plants dot the bottom of the run, with a depth ranging to about 15 feet. Fish are everywhere. The mill pond is considered one of America's premiere spots for record-size bream.

Along the run are two caves right together. The caves come together in a room about 30 feet down. Also along the run are Hole In The Wall cave and Gator Cave. You should not try the caves unless you are an advanced cave diver.

To get to Merritt's Mill Pond, go east from Marianna on U.S. 90 for just over a mile. Go left on Florida 71 for about a mile and turn right on Florida 164. Then turn right at the Blue Spring sign. In addition to the commercial area, there are a few fish camps and other spots where divers can reach the picturesque banks of the pond.

Morrison Spring

This is one of the area's larger springs and is about 40 miles from Panama City beaches. The spring basin is a half mile from the Choctawhatchee River and is circled by moss-laden cypress, making it a picture-postcard scene.

The spring's sides slope to an underwater bluff that cascades to about 50 feet. The spring also contains two caverns. One opening is at about 45 feet and is fairly large. The other opening, much smaller, is at 60 feet and divers can feel the flow of spring water coming out of this cavern. Divers report this cavern opens to a large room and depths of 90 feet have been attained in this cavern.

From U.S. 98 go north on Florida 79 to Ebro. Turn left on Florida 20 and travel approximately five miles. Turn right on Florida 81 toward the town of Ponce de Leon. Travel approximately 16 miles from the Florida 20- Florida 81 intersection and turn right on Florida 181. The spring area is about two miles from that turnoff, off the right side of the road at the end of a sand road. Signs point the way.

Heavy rains can flood this spring and make it undivable at certain times of the year. Check ahead to make sure it is open. There is a charge for diving.

Vortex Spring

This dive site is well developed commercially, offering a full-service dive shop, equipment rental, air, and even dormitory-style sleeping accommodations. Camping also is available.

Vortex is one of the southeast's most popular sites for check-out dives. Platforms have been stationed in several areas at varying depths for check-out procedures to be conducted.

Vortex pool is about 50 feet deep, and beyond that an underwater cave can be explored to a depth of about 125 feet.

Divers who have not visited Vortex in the past few years will be elated to learn that the spring has been cleared of hydrilla that had choked the spring basin in recent years and a layer of four-inch stones now covers the basin area which keeps the spring clear even with a large number of divers in the water.

In past years a lot of divers in the water stirred the bottom which quickly reduced visibility. That is now only a past memory.

In the spring basin, divers can swim into the cavern mouth, which has a 14-foot-high ceiling and is 80 feet across. This cavern extends back about 60 feet. Experience divers can continue another 300 feet through a garage-size tunnel to a dead end at a grate.

Divers with cave diving certification can arrange to swim beyond the grate to 1,500 feet and a depth of 135 feet.

Two man-made "caverns" were placed in the basin last year. These cement tunnels are huge drain pipes decorated with stalactites

No Waves
Deep Basin
*Cavern & Cave
Good Snorkel Run
Always Clear Water
Camping Year Round
With Permanent Line
Lodging for Dive Groups
Dormitory & Efficiency Rooms
*PROPER CERTIFICATION REQUIRED

NIGHT DIVING
LOTS OF FISH

VORTEX Spring INC.

4 Miles N. of Ponce de Leon, Fla., on Hwy. 81 N.
5 Miles from I-10 exit Route 2, Box 650, 32455
A/C (904) 836-4979
1-800-342-0640

and stalagmites to simulate a cavern dive. They range from six to 10 feet high and 15 feet wide in places.

Fresh water fish still are plentiful.

Water temperature is 68 degrees all the time, and visibility generally is about 200 feet.

A day of diving is $10. Snorkeling and swimming is $1.75 per day. Paddle boats, flat chairs and canoes are available for rent.

Vortex Springs is just north of Ponce de Leon, Fla., just off highway 81. Telephone: 1-800-342-0640.

Before scheduling a dive trip to the springs, watch the weather. If heavy rains have been moving through northwest Florida, call ahead to check spring conditions.

Some of these springs flood easily with murky runoff water. Others almost never turn cloudy.

In addition, the dirt roads to some of the non-commercial springs can turn into quagmires. Be careful not to get stuck.

The many caves and caverns found in these springs, usually carved from the soft limestone by the rush of spring water, are temptations. But resist the urge to explore unless you have a cave-trained guide or unless you are a certified cave diver. A failed light, pressing beyond experience and disorientation in a closed area has caused the death of more than one diver.

Spring water usually is cooler than gulf water and many divers favor at least a wetsuit jacket even in the warmest seasons.

All of the pools are ideal for underwater photography, and several are known for Indian and prehistoric fossil artifact hunting. Spear fishing of freshwater game fish is not allowed.

Divers peer into the opening of Cypress Spring, known for its strong flow of crystalline water
Photo courtesy of Harold Vickers, Cypress Spring

Spear Fishing/ Fish Identification

Spear fishing in fresh water has been severely limited for years, and limitations in salt water are increasing yearly—partly to protect swimmers and other sport divers, and partly to protect endangered species.

Still spear fishing opportunities in the northern Gulf of Mexico are phenomenal, particularly where it involves trophy size sport fish such as grouper, snapper and amberjack.

Always check local spear fishing regulation.

Spear fishermen find the northern Gulf of Mexico a great seafood factory. Some of America's finest table fare comes from these waters.

Equipment used in this region ranges from the super-simple hand spear or spear-and-sling to heavy-duty spear guns capable of knocking down a fish of more than a hundred pounds (if you hit it in the right place).

The fish divers most frequently go after are grouper, triggerfish, amberjack, flounder and snappers.

Be familiar with your equipment. Don't shoot fish that are too large for your spear gun to handle; and don't shoot fish that you are not experienced to cope with. Those may include sharks, moray eels, sting rays and barracuda.

When diving on a wreck, reef, artificial reef or oil rig where the fish have gathered, targets will be abundant. Furthermore, unless the fish have been spooked by heavy diver pressure, they usually will allow the diver to get extremely close.

The diver's main problem will be selecting the fish he wants to shoot and making sure he shoots the fish in a vital spot.

Before going spear fishing, divers should be competent in the following basics:

1. Know your gear. Most northern gulf dive shops do not rent spears or spear guns. So you probably will have to have your own. Determine the size fish your weapon is designed for and limit your ambitions to that size. Learn the spear's range and don't try to overextend.

2. Arm your spear gun only after you get in the water; disarm it before getting out.

3. Approach your quarry smoothly, quietly, without jerky motions or rapid breathing.

4. Keep your spear gun aimed forward so that once you have positioned your body for a shot, you can aim and fire quickly without excessive movement.

5. Aim for the fish's midline, just behind the gill plate. A broadside shot here will put a fish down.

6. Some divers will string several fish on their spear lines if they are in a large school of fish and plan to return to the boat within a few moments. This is an individual decision. Blood in the water attracts predators such as sharks and barracuda. Ideally, a spear fisherman should boat his catch as quickly as possible.

Following is a dictionary of fishes commonly found in the northern Gulf of Mexico. It does not include every species that a diver may encounter. Rather the dictionary emphasizes game fish that divers often seek to spear.

Amberjack

This large—to more than 100 pounds—member of the jack family is commonly found schooling over wrecks, high profile reefs and around rigs. Where you find one you usually will find others. The higher the profile of the structure, the more likely amberjack will be around, it seems. The fish is known for its fighting abilities; thus, if you do not hit a kill shot, be ready to hang on. Average weight is five to 15 pounds, but the range to more than 100 pounds. Greenish gray on the back and lighter on the belly, the amberjack is distinguished by a dark slash that runs through the fish's eye. Found year around. Food value, good.

Barracuda

This fish worries inexperienced divers only slightly less than sharks. After a couple of encounters, however, divers find that worry largely unfounded. These large, long, slender fish have an impressive array of sharp teeth—capable of lopping off an arm with a single swipe if they so choose. While they are more common around rigs, rocks and reefs, their presence does not warrant divers scurrying out of the water. Divers should keep an eye on them, and avoid wearing bright or flashy jewelry, particularly if the water is murky. There always is the chance that the barracuda will mistake the flash of jewelry for a wounded baitfish. While there have been rare reports of barracuda up to 10 feet long, even a five footer is rare. Some divers spear barracuda, but most do not. They are edible—if you are real hungry.

Black Drum

This drum, like others, is from the croaker family and gets its name from the loud drumming noise it can make by vibrating muscles and causing its air bladder to vibrate. The Black Drum is dusky with darker stripes when younger and more silvery with dark bands when older. It has a few barbels on its lower jaw. These fish live around rocks, oyster beds and pilings. They are found both in the bay and gulf. While a record Black Drum will be more than four-feet-long and weigh more than 150 pounds, the average is less than 10 pounds with two and three pounders common. Edible.

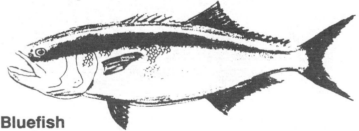

Bluefish

These fellows are in a class (biologically speaking) by themselves. In some ways they resemble pompano; in others, the sea basses. They range from bluish on the back to a whitish belly. It is an elongated fish—one to two feet long—with a forked tail and strong, snapping jaws with enough teeth to give you a nasty bite if you get an appendage in the wrong place. In the northern gulf these fish are commonly one to five pounders. If you encounter one in the 25-pound range you are getting close to record size. Blues are schooling fish, voracious eaters and gritty fighters. Blues can be found in the surf, channels, bays and gulf waters all year around. However, they seem most common in the fall, winter and spring. Bluefish are considered good eating by many, but they do not freeze well.

Blue Runner

Also known as hardtail, this smallish shallow-water member of the jack family is known as an important baitfish than it is as diver's quarry. Found around shallow jetties. The blue runner is greenish to bluish on the back and upper sides, shading to a yellowish-silver, and with translucent fins.

Bonito

Also called Little Tuna, this bloody-fleshed fish has been the disappointment of many a mackerel fisherman. This steely-blue and silver fighter is common in large schools in the northern gulf. Divers will see them thrashing along the surface, and as torpedo-fast missiles flashing through schools of bait fish around reefs, wrecks and rigs. Common at about five pounds, bonito can go to more than 20 pounds. Common in northern gulf waters from March through October. Almost never are used as people food.

Catfish

Divers encounter two species of salt-water catfish in northern gulf waters. The common sea catfish is the bad guy. It looks like a close relative of the fresh-water blue cat. Do not be fooled. The one-to two-pound sea catfish isa trash fish of no food value. Slimy, spiky fins can cause nasty punctures that always seem to get infected. They seem to be everywhere—in bays, around jetties, in the open gulf, on sandy bottoms and around structure. The good guy is the Gafftopsail Catfish. It is a fine food fish. The bluish-white Gafftopsail is common in bays, channels and inshore waters. They are more common in deeper water during the coldest part of winter. The Gafftopsail is distinguished by its long ribbon-like pectoral and dorsal fins. Two to five pounders are common.

Cobia

Also known as Ling and Lemonfish, this large fish is something of a loner. The Cobia averages 20 pounds or more and is found migrating the shoreline between mid-March and late May. After that, single Cobia are found over wrecks and reefs during warm weather. Color ranges from dark yellow-brown to a dark bluish-slate color on top, and shading to white on the belly. It sometimes has a dark stripe running from its eye to caudal fin. The fish is easily recognized by its flat head and protruding lower jaw. They are fine table fare.

Croaker

These fish are common in grass and around oyster beds, on sandy bottoms, along channels or near the beaches. They can be identified by a mouth slung just underneath a rounded nose, dark vertical bars running from their backs down their sides, and their small chin barbels. They average about a pound; a four- to five-pounder is a prize. Croakers get their name from the croaking noise they make. Divers frequently encounter schools of croakers. They are a decent food fish.

Dolphin

Don't get this excellent game and food fish mixed up with the mammal of the same name. The dolphin is one of the northern gulf's most colorful fishes, looking like a rainbow of blues, greens and yellows. The colored stripes run the length of their long, sleek bodies. The male differs from the female in that he has an extremely high forehead, giving a squared-off look. School dolphin range from one to five pounds, and grow up to tackle busters of more than 50 pounds. Divers see them schooling in open water, around buoys, grass mats and tide lines. They are too fast to spear. Excellent food value.

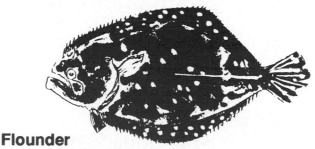

Flounder

This flatfish comes from a large family of fishes that swim and lie on their sides. A flounder's top side is a mottled brown and can change color to match that of its surroundings. Its other side (the one that lays on the sand) is white. This important game and food fish is a year-around resident of the northern gulf, moving into shallow water—sometimes right up to the beach—in warmer weather, and into deeper water during cooler months. The flounder averages a pound or two and can grow to over 15 pounds. These are favorite targets for spear fishermen, mainly for their outstanding food value. Lying still on the bottom, half covered with sand, they are sitting ducks for a diver with a spear.

Gafftopsail Catfish

See Catfish.

Grouper

There are 40 or more species of grouper, and a number of them live in northern gulf waters. There are spotted ones, red ones, gray ones, black ones and blotched ones; small ones and giant ones. They have common characteristics—they are generally of a similar shape, have large mouths akin to the largemouth bass, a dorsal fin that is spiny in the front and soft in the back and a continuous lateral line. And they all are tasty food fish. Several of the species also are favorite spear fishing targets since they are large and usually easy to get close to. They range from the giant Jewfish that can weigh more than 700 pounds to several species that run less than a pound. Most common to northern gulf divers are the gag (commonly called black grouper), red, scamp and yellowfin to name several. Virtually all groupers are bottom feeders and can be found around structure that provides cover. They are found year around.

Ground Mullet

Actually is a cousin of the whiting and not a real mullet at all. Unlike the silver or surf whiting found exclusively in the surf, this species is light brown, sometimes with darker splotches, and lives in bays. It is a slender fish with a weak tail, has an underslung mouth, with a barbel on its chin. It averages about a foot long and weighs about a pound. They are more interesting parts of the landscape on bay dives than spear fishing targets, however they are excellent to eat.

Hardtail

See Blue Runner.

Jack Crevalle

This inshore fighter, pound for pound, is one of the fightingest fish in the gulf. It is a light olive-green color on the back, shading to gray, gold and yellow along the sides to the belly. It has a black spot on the gill cover and a deeply forked tail. It has a heftier body and blunter head than other members of the jack family. Commonly encountered over wrecks and other structure. Jacks range to more than 30 pounds. They frequent the northern gulf in the spring, summer and fall. Food value, poor.

Jewfish

See Grouper.

Lizard Fish

Divers don't hunt for this fish, but they always seem to come across them, laying on the bottom waiting for an unsuspecting meal to swim by. It is a vile little fish with a toothy wide mouth and ill disposition. Itt lives both in bays and off shore, usually on sandy bottom but near vicinity of structure where baitfish gather. It reaches about a foot in length, is a mottled brown and has a flat, pointed head. Food value, none.

Mackerel

The northern gulf is the seasonal home to several species of these important sport fish. Divers frequently encounter mackerels, most often schooling around jetties or near the surface in the open gulf. Almost never do divers attempt to spear mackerel. They are too swift for a clean shot. Jetty and shore divers encounter Spanish and northern mackerel (local term) that patrol the near shore waters. They occasionally encounter a king mackerel in close, but more often the king is found farther off shore. Further off shore the Wahoo is found.

The **northern mackerel**—as it is locally known—is a small fish, about a pound and a half on average, is a metallic blue above the lateral line, with a golden sheen and light green cast. It has a mottled, lined look on its top half and is whitish-silvery below. They are thicker bodied, side to side, than the other local mackerels.

Spanish mackerel is one of the first mackerels to arrive in the northern gulf each spring, and is highly sought after by fishermen. It is generally larger than the northern mackerel, but smaller than the king mackerel. The Spanish mackerel have yellow spots on their sides and a gently curved lateral line They average two to four pounds, and occasionally exceed 10 pounds.

King mackerel arguably are *the* most important sport fish of the northern gulf. Anglers by the thousand troll inshore waters in the warm months for these sleek, silvery battlers. The migratory fish makes its way up the Florida peninsula, arriving in northern gulf waters usually in April. Off Louisiana some kings winter around the oil rigs, and generally are among the largest ones found in the northern gulf. The king mackerel is black to navy blue on the back, shading to silver on the sides and white on the belly. Kings average six or eight pounds, but can range to 50 pounds. All the mackerel are considered good food fish. They are best when fresh, not frozen.

Wahoo are offshore mackerel that are spotted by divers only rarely. They are distinguished from other mackerel by a long dorsal fin and wavy vertical lines along the body. They average 15 to 20 pounds, and are fairly common.

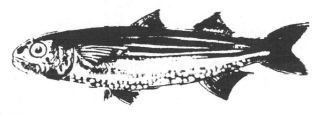

Moray Eel

Rocks, wrecks, reefs and rigs of the northern gulf are home for a variety of moray eels. They are slick-bodied, shy, toothy eels that spend most of their time hiding in holes and cracks—easing out for an occasional unsuspecting meal that happens to swim by. They also are known by their large mouths, filled with needle-like teeth. Do not attempt to handle a moral eel. While the average moray is less than two feet, some have been known to grow to more than six feet. Morays are not considered food fish.

Mullet

This important food fish is commonly seen during bay and shore dives, traveling in schools near the surface in fairly shallow water. The mullet averages around two pounds and can be found ranging to near 10 pounds. It roams the surf and bays in schools. Mullet are more a part of the near-shore scenery than they are spear fishing targets. While mullet are tasty when cooked fresh, their flesh is soft and does not freeze well.

Octopus

This creature, much maligned as a sea monster in movies and novels, is another of those animals that you do not spear, but rather just enjoy watching as it works its way around its watery home. They have a soft central body, with eight arms radiating from the center. Its arms are lined with suction cups. On the underside is a mouth with a beak. It lives both in bays and the open gulf. Most commonly it is found around piers, rocks, coral or other structure. The octopus ranges in color from a yellow-brown to a pinkish brown, and has the ability to quickly change colors when excited, frightened or feeding. The meat, particularly the tentacles, is edible.

Pinfish (choffer)

These bright blue and yellow striped fish fill the water around jetties, with divers spotting larger ones around reefs several miles off shore. It is a common panfish, four to five inches long, and found year around. They are a dominant part of the scenery on shore, pier or jetty dives. They have a fairly strong iodine taste. A slightly larger and less common species of pinfish, the Spottail Pinfish, is found in the same areas, and is somewhat more palatable as a food fish.

Pompano

Some say this is the finest eating fish that swims. Others seek the pompano for its sporting fight. Divers spot the pompano on surf and jetty dives, patrolling the shallows for sand fleas. It is a roundish fish, silver to yellow-gold with a deep forked tail. It ranges from less than a pound to slightly more than two pounds. Anything over five pounds is a trophy. They are found beginning around the first of May. A shy fish that divers do not go after with a spear gun.

Red Drum (Redfish, Channel Bass)

This fish is perhaps the most famous and most sought after of the croakers. It is a goldish-red color, with a heavy body, underslung mouth and a dark spot near the tail. They are the largest and noisiest of the croakers, with school reds averaging three to eight pounds, and bull reds commonly running 15 to 20 pounds. The red is a bottom feeder, found in the surf and, more frequently, in channels and around piers. They are in northern gulf waters year around, but are most common in the fall, winter and early spring. Due to heavy commercial harvesting, there are stringent limits on the size and number of reds that can be taken. Check local regulations. Food value, good.

Remoras

Also known as shark suckers, but that does not mean a shark is lurking right around the corner. The silver, black and gray remora averages a foot to two feet. It is a seagoing parasite, and easily recognized by the flat suction plate atop its head. This fish can be found around floating debris (they will hang around a dive boat if it stays anchored for any amount of time), or attached to sharks, swordfish or other large fish. They are not considered edible.

Sharks

Yes, they swim in northern gulf waters. Yes, they have sharp teeth. Yes, they will make your heart beat a little faster if you bump into one while diving. Just remember, they are *always* there, so shy that they rarely get close enough for the diver to ever see them. Normally they will retreat if approached. Do not put sharks in situations where they feel threatened—they will react like other animals. A diver finding himself in the presence of a shark that postures aggressively, should get out of the water.

Some sharks are more aggressive than others, but all should be treated with respect. The most famous, the great white, is a shark that divers just don't see. Those spotted in the gulf have been far off shore in deep water.

Sharks that divers may encounter in the northern gulf include:

Atlantic Sharpnose. A grayish shark with irregular spots. Grows to about three feet.

Black Tip. This gray-black shark can be identified by the black tips of its fins. It averages five feet and grows to 10. It is considered a good game fish.

Blue. Bluish-gray on the back, shading to white. It averages 10 feet and has been reported to 25 feet. The younger ones have black-tipped fins.

Bonnethead. Easily identified by the shovel-shaped head. Can be found near shore and in bays. A bottom feeder that grows to about three feet.

Brown or Sandbar. Grows to about eight feet. A bottom feeder that divers are most likely to encounter on open gulf structure.

Bull. Easily recognized by blunt, rounded nose. Heavy body, dark gray to brown. An abundant shark that ranges from offshore into bays.

Dogfish. This is a fisherman's pest. It grows to about five feet, is grayish on top and lighter underneath.

Dusky. Can exceed 10 feet, but rather slender. It is common near shore as well as off shore. Grayish-brownish on top shading to white underneath.

Hammerhead. This shark averages around eight feet, and has been reported up to 20 feet. It is grayish on top and lighter below. The eyes are located at either end of a cross bar on the head.

Lemon. A common near-shore species. Can reach 11 feet at maturity and weigh 200 pounds. It is yellowish-brown, with darker splotches. The belly is a lighter yellow.

Mako. Averages eight feet and can reach more than 10 feet and weigh a half ton. Considered a good game fish. Dark blue on the back, shading to white on the belly.

Sand Tiger Shark. Common longer than 10 feet, and can grow to 15. Frequents coastal waters, particularly around reefs. Easily identified by splattered splotch appearance.

Tiger. Averages eight feet and can range to about 15, weighing more than a half ton. It is light brown with spotted fins and vertical stripes. The stripes tend to disappear in older tigers.

Actually, only an expert could positively identify many species, and then only after close examination. Divers probably are not going to stop to examine the fine points when they encounter a shark.

They all have sharp teeth and rough, sandpaper-like skin. The better part of valor is to leave them alone and tell your stories about the hair-raising encounter.

Sheepshead

This member of the porgy family has a typical panfish shape, although it is a larger member of the species. The fish has dark vertical stripes on a lighter background. Common in the three- to six-pound range, and frequently found in bays, channels and near-shore structure. The sheepshead is a favorite of spear fishermen for its approachability and edibility.

Snappers

Probably the most prized table fare of the gulf bottom fish, the snappers became more and more rare through the 1980s. In the past few years, however, size and creel limits have resulted in a noticeable comeback. While the red snapper is by far the most sought after, close to a dozen different kinds roam gulf waters.

Snapper common to the northern gulf include:

Red Snapper populations are centered in the Gulf of Mexico. These fish are a smooth red on back, shading to white below, without lines or stripes. These bottom fish are found around reefs, wrecks and rigs. They average one to six pounds, and can exceed 40 pounds. Check current size and catch limits.

Gray Snapper is a smaller snapper, averaging a pound and a half, and almost never reaching 10 pounds. These fish are found in bays, around jetties and in the open gulf. While some gray snapper may have a hint of red, they are more commonly gray or grayish green. This fish also is referred to as Black Snapper.

Lane Snapper. This snapper shares the common snapper shape, and has the red color of the red snapper. However it is easily distinguished from the red snapper by several yellowish stripes that run the length of the fish. This snapper can be found around reefs, and on sandy bottoms from fairly shallow water to great depths. While these fish average around a foot long, they can grow to a foot and a half.

Vermilion Snapper (Beeliner, Mingo) is a deep red colored snapper, with a slightly more elongated body than the red snapper. It has a shorter nose and more upturned mouth than the other snappers. It is a staple of the northern gulf charter fishing fleets where heavy stringers of this snapper are brought in from each trip. The average is just under a foot in length and weighing less than a pound, but can range to four or five pounds. It is abundant around most open gulf structure. Food value is quite good when prepared fresh.

White Snapper. This common reef fish is not a snapper at all, but rather one of a half dozen or more members of the porgy family. These fish can range from a faintly pink to white to white with a green cast. Some have blue and green coloration on the nose. The average a pound or so, but can range to 10 pounds. They are easy targets for spear fishermen. While they have the general snapper shape, these fish are easily identified as porgies by the molar-like teeth.Excellent table fare.

Spadefish

This member of a tropical fish family is shaped similar to the triggerfish. It is silver with prominent vertical stripes. The bigger the fish gets, the lighter the stripes. The spadefish averages just over a pound, and grows to more than five pounds. It lives around wrecks, reefs, piers, seawalls and jetties. It is a frequent and dramatic sight for divers as they pass over structure in large schools. It is a target for spear fishermen, and is considered good eating.

Speckled Trout (Spotted Weakfish)

This fish is shaped something like freshwater trout. It is darker on the back, shading to silver on the belly. It is spotted on the upper half. Speckled trout average one to five pounds. They are found in bays, inlets and brackish rivers. They are found in the northern gulf year around, concentrated in deeper holes in the winter and scattered in summer. These are skittish fish, hardly ever speared. The speck is a soft-fleshed fish that is good fresh.

Stingray

Divers come across stingrays or some other type ray on almost every dive. They range from bays to the open gulf. With wide, flat bodies rays frequently lay on the bottom waiting for lunch to swim by. They are easily avoided by divers—a good plan. Stingrays have several sharp poisonous spines near the base of the tail. These spines cause a nasty wound. The stingray and relatives are common year around.

Triggerfish

This rounded fish is easy to identify by its gray thick rough skin and by its three dorsal spines. One of the spines "unlocks" the others so they can be depressed and folded into a notch on the fish's back--thus, the trigger of the triggerfish. It averages about a pound, but can exceed 10 pounds. Triggerfish can be found around structure in bays, channels and in the open gulf. They are nibblers with nasty dispositions, known to nip divers with their strong, squirrel-like teeth. Divers have come to appreciate the triggerfish because it is an easy spearfishing target and because of the excellent flavor of its firm, white meat.

Tuna

They don't haul them in over the rails like you see in the commercials. But there are plenty of tuna in the gulf. Only a few, however, range inshore enough to be seen by divers. The skipjack and blackfin tunas are the most likely to be encountered. Like all tunas, they are red-fleshed, fast moving, muscular fish constantly moving in search of food. All are extremely rare in sport diver range.

White Trout

This fish looks like a smaller version of the Speckled Trout, but without the coloring or spots. It is white or silvery and generally runs from slightly less than a pound to about three pounds. It is common in bays and channels year around. Spear fishermen do not seek this fish, but often discover it as part of the scenery of a bay or jetty dive. The trout's meat is decent when cooked fresh.

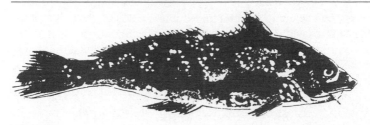

Whiting

Summer snorkelers see schools of these fish in the surf and around jetties. They grow to about five pounds. Most average about a pound. They are long, thin fish, silvery white, with an underslung mouth and a barbel on the chin. They are exclusively surf fish and quite common. They are excellent table fare.

Shell Collecting/ Shell Identification

Snorkelers, particularly from Phillips Inlet in the Florida peninsula westward, complain about the lack of shells in the shallow surf. It is well founded.

Through the western panhandle, surf action coupled with sandbar structure allow only a few small shells to make it to shore intact. Further west, off the Mississippi and Louisiana coasts, the many barrier islands and muddier bottom bring in a number of snail-like shellfish, but not the prize shells that the eastern gulf is known for.

The situation is no indication of a lack of shells in the area. Throughout the Florida panhandle and Alabama coast east of Mobile Bay, and the gulf side of the barrier islands, snorkelers can find a variety of shells

Off Louisiana and Mississippi, shells gather around the artificial reefs and oil rigs just as they do around the reefs of the eastern end of this region.

The real gulf treasures are found around the wrecks, rigs, artificial and natural reefs. The crustaceans and other plant life that attaches to the structure draws the shellfish to feed. From huge conchs and whelks to tiny, brilliant cowries, these areas are treasure chests for shell hunters.

A keen eye is required. The shells you see in tourist shops have been cleaned and oiled. In their natural state many of them have a completely different appearance. Some are covered with plant growth; others, like cowries, cannot be seen when the animal completely covers the shell much of the time.

A careful explorer will quickly adjust to the different appearances. Just take along a cloth or mesh bag for your find.

Shells some in two varieties: bivalves and univalves. Bivalves are shells with two sides, and are hooked together by a hinge at the back. Univalves consist of a single shell, usually swirl shaped.

Both shells are the homes of animals of a zoological family called mollusks. If you find a shell that is "alive," the mollusk will be inside. These animals can move around, taking their shells with them wherever they go, breathe and excrete lime to make their shells grow. A few move only when they are very young, then attach themselves to rocks, coral or other objects to live out their lives.

Here are a few tips on preparing shells for display. Dead bivalves need no care. However, live bivalves and all univalves, except for the tiniest ones, need to be boiled in water.

Put tiny and extremely fragile shells in formaldehyde.

The boiling or formaldehyde will kill the animal inside so it can then be removed easily.

You won't be able to pull the animal out without damaging the shell otherwise. And, allowing the animal to die and decompose will leave you with a shell that will smell—seemingly forever.

Once boiled, bivalves will open and the animal can easily be scraped out. Univalve animals can be pulled out with a hooked piece of wire or bent clothes hanger. Univalves should be boiled whether the original animal lives there or not. These shells are favorite homes for hermit crabs and even an occasional small octopus that you might not notice at first glance.

Use a fingernail file or dull knife to gently scrape away any crustaceans clinging to the outside of the shells.

After cleaning the shells, soak them in a mild chlorine solution (1/4 liquid chlorine bleach, 3/4 water is fine) and then in muriatic acid. They should be soaked two to four hours.

Once the shells have dried (not in direct sunlight) give them a light coat of oil and they will keep their natural color and luster almost forever. Baby oil works well.

If your shells appear to be fading after a few months, give them a fresh coat of oil and their original colors will return.

Some collectors dip their shells in liquid plastic, shellac or varnish. This is not necessary to preserve their color and is not recommended.

Following is an illustrated listing of shells that may be found along northern gulf beaches or in coastal waters within reach of sport divers. Some are common. Others are found only in deep water.

Angel Wing

Found occasionally along the shore. Lives buried in mud and sand. Shells are fragile, up to six to eight inches long.

Arks (Turkey Wing)

Can be found along beaches. Bright, reddish brown, with prominent ribs. A heavy shell. Two to three inches.

Augers

Various types. Some are found near the beach; others are found only in deeper water. Some are brightly colored; others gray to white. Most are sand dwellers.

Bonnets

Occasionally found along beaches, but rarely unbroken. Fragile. Most often found offshore. To three inches.

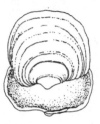

Buttercup Lucine

They are members of a tropical clam family, living on sandy and mud bottoms, in both shallow and moderate depth waters. Thin, but strong shell. May be found near beach. To two inches.

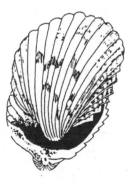

Cockles

Heart shaped, with strong radiating ribs. Live in shallow sand and mud and are common along certain beaches. Perhaps the most commonly-found treasure of the beach collector. To five inches.

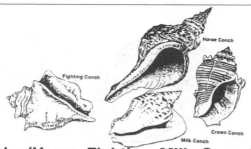

Conchs (Horse, Fighting, Milk, Crown)

Found both along beaches, in bay waters and in deeper water, with larger species usually in deeper water. Found on sandy bottoms. They are the shells frequently stacked up for sale outside roadside shell stands. From two to three inches for smaller species to more than a foot for larger varieties.

Clams

Found in bays usually. One to five inches. Heavy, whitish-gray shell.

Cones

Only a few varieties of this large tropical group are available along the northern gulf. Found among rocks and coral, usually in deeper water. Bright colored in yellows and browns on a white background. From one to three inches.

Coquinas

Found along the shore in large numbers and a variety of colors. Live just beneath the sand's surface at the water's edge. In some areas they are used to make chowder. Up to one inch, usually less.

Measled Cowry

Atlantic
Deer Cowry

Cowries (Measled and Atlantic Deer)

Not plentiful. Normally found in deeper water around reefs and rocks. Shells appear highly polished. From one to four inches.

Fusinus

Also known as spindle shells. Live on sandy bottoms and travel in pairs. Not common. A collector's item because of its long graceful shape. To four or five inches.

Jewel Boxes

Found offshore around rocks, reefs, rigs and wrecks. These are delicate and sometimes brilliantly colored. From one to three inches.

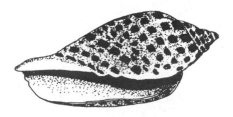

Junonia

Normally lives in deeper water, however very rarely washes onto beach. Not common. Four to five inches.

Lion's Paw

A type of scallop, with a strong, heavy shell. Found in deeper water and is a collector's favorite. Three to five inches.

Moon Shell

Several varieties, with most common being the Atlantic Shark Eye. Found on beaches, in surf and in bays. Common. To two inches.

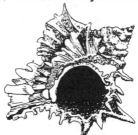

Murex

Common in shallow water, usually in bays and channels on

muddy or grassy bottoms. There are more than 1,000 species in the family, with several in the northern gulf area. They are threats to oyster beds. From one to five inches.

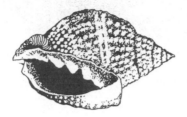

Nutmegs

Found both near shore and in deeper water. Has strong spiral teeth on inner lip of shell. To two inches.

Olives

Related to cowries, can be found on the beach; common in shallow sandy surf at certain times of the year. Polished appearance; olive green color. Two to three inches.

Oysters

Common. So common that discarded shells are used in place of gravel in some areas. An important food fish. Found in bays, on pilings, reefs, piers, etc. Not a collector's item.

Pen Shell

Common. Found alive, buried in shallow soft sand or mud, usually in bays. Anchored by hair-like byssus. Great care must be taken loosening them from the sand. To more than 12 inches.

Queen Helmet

This cousin of the conch is found in deeper water. Shell is heavy, triangular and thick lipped. Three to six inches.

Scallops

Bay scallop is most common. Shells are found on beach, in bays and in surf. Live shells found in bay grass beds. Colors vary from black to white, and shades in between, plus calico and reddish brown. One to three inches.

Spiny Oysters

Also known as Thorny Oysters. Not true oysters. Have a rich and varied color. Usually found near reefs and wrecks in deeper water. Fairly common. To six inches.

Star Shells

Found in deeper water. Rays extend from the swirls of this univalve, thus the name Star Shell. To two inches.

Sun Dials

Most common in deeper water, and on sand bottom. Shell resembles a winding staircase. To two inches.

Top Shells

Found in deeper water. To two inches.

Triton (Trumpet, Hairy)

Found near structure in deeper water. In some areas of the world members of the Triton shell family are used to make trumpets by cutting off the end of the shell's spire or by drilling a hole in the side of the shell. The Hairy Triton gets its name from the "hairs" covering the outside of the shell. Common on reefs. Trumpet to 11 inches. Hairy to four inches.

Tulips

Found on shore, in bays and surf. Several species. Common. Three to five inches.

Tun

Found in deeper water. Large, thin, rounded shell. Two to 10 inches.

Volutes

See Junonia.

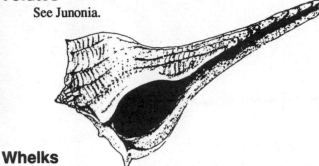

Whelks

A large species. Found on the beach, in shallow and deeper water, gulf and bays. Common. Three to 16 inches. At times of year, collectors find their egg cases along the beach, sometimes with many tiny shells inside.

Wentletraps

Also known as Staircase or Ladder Shells. Delicate, thin shell. Live in deeper water. One inch.

*Panama City waters
give up a 65-pound
black grouper*
Photo by Bill Ziel
Courtesy of Hydrospace

*Triggerfish, sheepshead and jacks cruise the encrusted
beams of a northern gulf oil rig.*
Photo courtesy of Captain J's dive shop, Destin, Fla.

Acknowledgements

No book gets done without the help of many generous folks who share their time, knowledge and talents. Operators of every dive shop listed in this book contributed significantly.

In addition, thanks also should go to:
Captain Mark Miller of Gautier, Miss., who spent many hour charting Mississippi coast dive spots. In addition to dive charters, Captain Miller is one of the area's most talented charter fishermen. If you plan to fish off the Mississippi coast, give him a call at (601)497-1950.

Captain Bill Tant of Birmingham and Panama City, one of the southeast's diving pioneers, and owner of Southern Skin Diver's Supply. Bill taught me to dive and to appreciate the underwater world.

Cover Photos

Front cover, upper right: A diver watches bluegill bream in the crystal clear waters of Vortex Spring near the northwest Florida town of Ponce de Leon. Photo courtesy of Gulf Coast Divers in Mobile, Alabama.

Front cover, center: Photographer Tanya Murphy captures the myriad of life over one of Panama City, Florida's wrecks. Photo courtesy of Tanya Murphy and Hydrospace Dive Shop.

Back cover, top: A large school of grunts gather around a reef near the Liberty Ship wreck, about six miles southwest of East Pass at Destin, Florida. A squirrelfish, brown and white striped, lurks near a large outcropping encrusted with colorful corals.

Back cover, bottom: Spearfishermen stalk their quarry in the web of a Louisiana oil rig, while schools of fish swarm around them.
Both back cover photos are courtesy of Captain J's dive shop in Destin, Florida.